ALAN NUNN MAY:
The Atom Spy and MI5

ALAN NUNN MAY:
The Atom Spy and MI5

JOHN H. SMITH

ALAN NUNN MAY
The Atom Spy and MI5
John H. Smith

Published by Aspect Design 2012
Malvern, Worcestershire, United Kingdom.

Designed and Printed by Aspect Design
89 Newtown Road, Malvern, Worcs. WR14 1PD
United Kingdom
Tel: 01684 561567
E-mail: books@aspect-design.net
Website: www.aspect-design.net

All Rights Reserved.
Copyright © 2013 John H. Smith

John Smith has asserted his moral right
to be identified as the author of this work.

The right of John H. Smith to be identified as the author
of this work has been asserted in accordance with
Section 77 of the Copyright, Designs and Patents Act 1988.

This book is sold subject to the condition that it shall not, by way of trade or otherwise, be lent, resold, hired out or otherwise circulated without the publisher's prior consent in any form of binding or cover other than that in which it is published and without a similar condition including this condition being imposed on the subsequent purchaser.

A copy of this book has been deposited with the British Library Board

Cover Design Copyright © 2012 Aspect Design

ISBN 978-1-908832-23-8

Paper used in the printing of this book has been sourced from
well-managed and credibly certified forests.

For Estelle

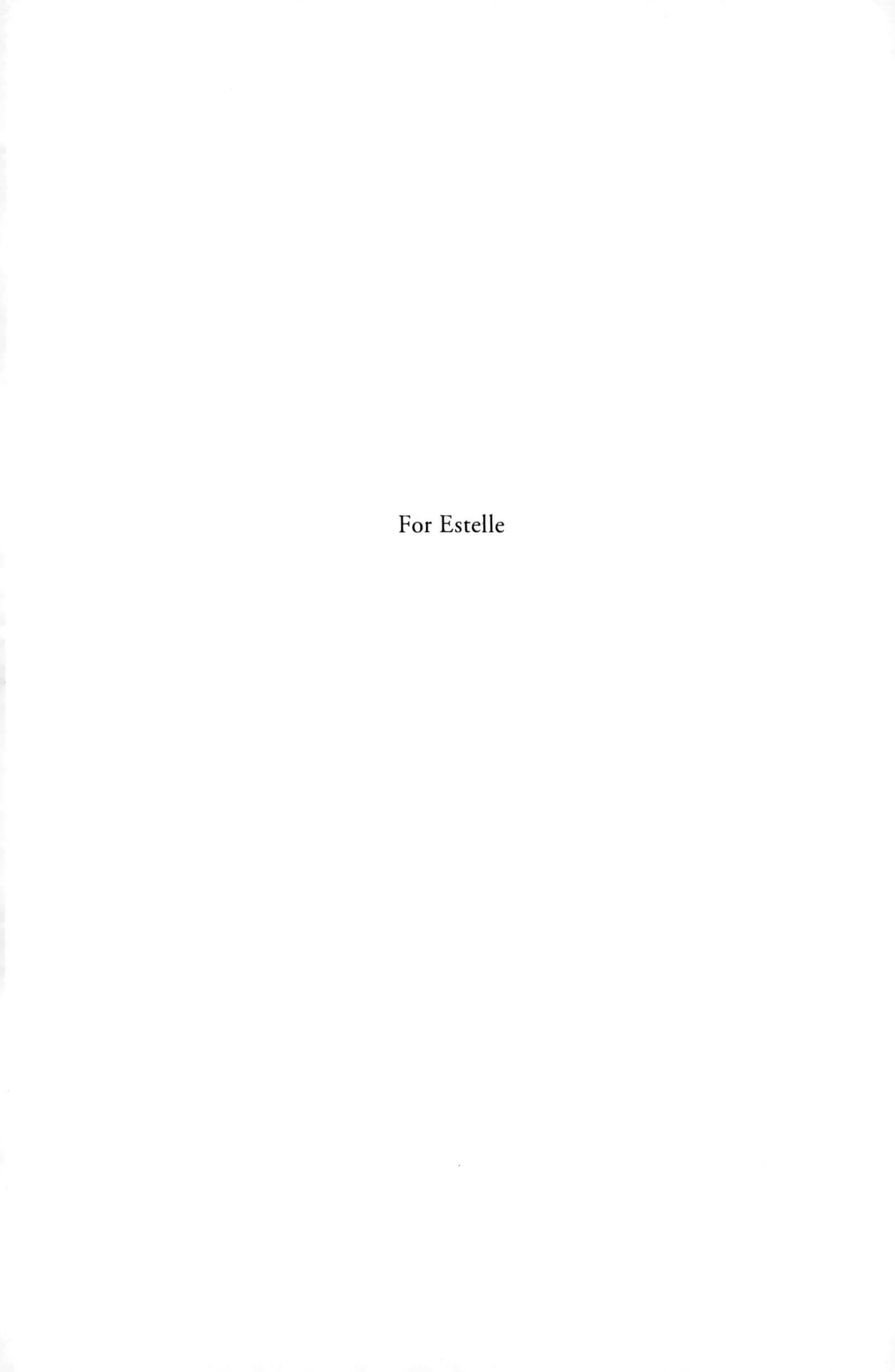

CONTENTS

Introduction 9
Chapter One 11
Chapter Two 20
Chapter Three 29
Chapter Four 34
Chapter Five 38
Chapter Six 43
Chapter Seven 48
Chapter Eight 61
Chapter Nine 74
Chapter Ten 80
Chapter Eleven 89
Chapter Twelve 96
Illustrations 110
Chapter Thirteen 113
Chapter Fourteen 122
Chapter Fifteen 126
Chapter Sixteen 139
Chapter Seventeen 143
Chapter Eighteen 154
Chapter Nineteen 161
Chapter Twenty 172
Chapter Twenty-One 181
Epilogue 192

INTRODUCTION

I have pursued my interest in Alan Nunn May over several years by virtue of his family's connection with the house I live in and his links with Barnt Green. The more I investigated the factors involved in his story the more I became absorbed in wanting to retell it.

In 2011, Paul Broda, Alan Nunn May's stepson released his book *Scientist Spies*. This is a memoir of Alan Nunn May's life and that of his father and mother Engelbert and Hildegarde Broda.

After some deliberation I decided to continue to publish the information I had collected as a record of my time spent in researching a fascinating topic. Much of the information I had gathered was not included in Paul Broda's book because he had to devote space to the fascinating lives of his mother and father. He had possession of family papers and letters to which I did not have access. Inevitably there are passages of this book which cover the same ground as *Scientist Spies*. I have made extensive use of the files held by the National Archives many of which could not be included in that publication. I amended my text to include major gaps in Nunn May's life of which I had no knowledge, but have chosen not to repeat many of the stories and the scientific detail.

I have been able to recount a story which highlights the operational workings of MI5 in the forties and fifties, the tensions between the United States government and the United Kingdom, legal deliberations, and the internal prevarications of our civil service.

I have tried to show that Alan Nunn May's completion of a prison sentence for his misdemeanours was only a prelude to his trying to overcome numerous obstacles during the rest of his life. His misdeeds had longstanding ramifications for his family, friends, working colleagues and other innocent parties.

John H. Smith

CHAPTER ONE

Alan Nunn May was born in Birmingham on May 2, 1911. His father Walter Frederick, was a brass founder and his mother Mary, often referred to as Minnie, came from Truro in Cornwall. They lived at Park Hill in Moseley, a suburb of Birmingham; but by 1913 Alan's parents had moved to Blackwell Road, Barnt Green, Worcestershire, and eventually to a semi-detached house in Sandhills Road, again in Barnt Green. This is an attractive large village about twelve miles to the south of Birmingham. Alan had two older brothers, Ralph and Edward and a sister Mary.

Alan suffered frequently from pneumonia as a child and was given special attention. Long periods of ill health resulted in him receiving his education from governesses and the local vicar. He went on to be educated at King Edward VI School, New Street, Birmingham. The school records show that his father paid eighteen pounds per term for his schooling during the years 1925–1927, but this ceased when he became a Foundation Scholar in 1928. This was a result of a downturn in the family's fortunes. The family had enjoyed a prominent social life in Barnt Green, where they played a major part in musical productions, including Gilbert and Sullivan concerts, as well as membership of the church choir. Alan played the piano and was able to help out with family rehearsals.

At the end of the 1914–18 war the family firm's premises was damaged by fire and Birmingham City Council refused permission to rebuild on the site. They eventually rebuilt elsewhere but in doing so incurred substantial loans. The business restarted but the post war boom had, by this time ended and the firm collapsed. Alan's father and his elder brother Edward, were removed from their own firm by the other directors. Edward found another job and became successful, whereas their father invested unsuccessfully in a milk distribution business and eventually became a representative for other metal firms. The changes necessitated moving to a semi detached house in Sandhills Road, Barnt Green.

These events had a profound influence on Alan. It now seemed that he had a responsibility to make his own way in life and needed to redouble his efforts by studying even harder at school. Alan gravitated towards physics as his main subject closely followed by mathematics. Alongside him were other very able pupils and they drove each other on in the mastery of mathematical problems. Alan had the study of physics more or less to himself and was soon studying aspects of relativity and books by Rutherford and Geiger.

In the vicinity of the school was the Birmingham Subscription Library. This contained books written by many of the day's radicals, such as Bertrand Russell and Bernard Shaw as well as the classics of English literature. It also contained a collection of gramophone and sheet music. Alan was to say in later life that the library had a major role in formulating his ideas and thinking.

He played an active part in the school Debating Society, where he opposed the motion, "That the Englishman's Conservatism in Dress is a National Asset." He told the House, 'What a delightful form of dress he could invent if he were given the chance. The chief absurdity of modern clothes was the enormous number of pockets, their only use of course was that they might hold enormous quantities of Cadbury's chocolate.'

On a separate occasion in a debate with the girl's school, he proposed the motion that, "School Life is a Misery". It was defeated.

In a debate with the headmaster in the chair, he seconded the motion that, "This House Deplores the Defeatist Tendencies in England at the Present Day". His remarks as a boy of eighteen, bearing in mind the political situation at the time, were interesting. Politics he said, 'should follow the advice of Sir John Reith, who said that he would not give the public what it wants but what it ought to have. The thing that mattered was not what a man believed but what he did not believe. Defeatism was the moral cowardice of degeneracy.' The motion was defeated. In a subsequent account of members of the Debating Society, Alan Nunn May was referred to as the most popular speaker of the society. He could produce laughter from the most serious of motions although the critic commented that he ought to speak a little louder.

A former neighbour, whose garden backed on to their house, once asked Alan's mother why the light seemed to remain on for so long in the upstairs bedroom. She replied that Alan was a quiet, diligent boy and was studying very hard and the world would one day know of his ability.

He was also a prefect and was photographed alongside fellow pupil, J. Enoch Powell. He matriculated in 1926 and in 1929 began preparation for entry examinations to Cambridge. The school set mock examination papers every Saturday morning, to enhance their pupils chances as there was great rivalry with other schools to secure scholarship places at Oxford and Cambridge.

Alan was successful and was awarded a Minor Scholarship at Trinity Hall, Cambridge. Alan's father had wanted him to become an accountant but Alan was relieved not to take that career choice.

Before going up to University, Alan had an opportunity to extend the breadth of his reading and began to question the ideas held by his parents and the older generation, particularly relating to the causes of the Second World War and the British Establishment.

By this time, one of Alan's brothers Ralph, had already been at the University of Birmingham and had been President of the National Union of Students in 1923. He was subsequently to make a career for himself in the film industry. The eldest brother Edward, was successful as a Company Director in a paint manufacturing firm.

The 1920s had been a turbulent political period in Britain. By the time Alan Nunn May was due to leave school in 1930 he was nineteen years of age, with a growing distrust of the political establishment. In terms of his career decisions and future political leanings, it is worth reflecting on some of the events and politics of that period which were to influence both himself and his future colleagues.

His older brothers would have been aware of the problems created by the 1914–18 war. The death toll had decimated an enormous swathe of men from all classes of society. It had robbed Britain of much of its future leadership and manpower. That war had been expected to lead to a better future for the citizens of Great Britain. The 1920s were to disappoint any expectations of a new Britain. Britain's influence as a significant power in the world had diminished and it was clinging on to the perception that its Victorian successes would continue as of right. Britain's industry had failed to modernise and keep pace with competing nations. Despite a successful coming together of social classes in wartime, the social and class structure had changed very little afterwards. The aristocracy saw little difference in their economic situation and no need to change. The war had also been devastating for them and it was time to throw off the shackles and have a good time, whilst they still had the money to do so.

The political landscape saw the emergence of the Labour Party which carried high hopes of a new mandate for the future. They formed governments in 1924 and in 1929 but they were unable to arrest a precipitous economic decline, mass unemployment, widespread poverty and the General Strike of 1926. In the face of such a depressing social and economic downturn, science was beginning to make its mark with astonishing developments in atomic physics. It remained the case however, that the leading public schools saw little to change their view that science was something of a backwater which provided little opportunity for personal advancement. The traditional route through the Classics or Greats at Oxford and Cambridge and onwards through politics and the diplomatic service was where true influence lay.

Alan's breadth of reading in his last years at school was already changing his political ideas from those of his parents. His elder brother Edward, seemed to be gregarious and commercially successful and survived the 1914–18 war. He must have had something to say about it all to his younger brother. He had been a lieutenant in the Royal Field Artillery in 1919, was awarded the Military Cross in the Honours List and continued his service in the Territorial Army advancing to

Lieutenant Colonel.

Alan left King Edward VI School, on 28 July 1930 and went up to Trinity Hall, Cambridge on an Open Scholarship taking Part I of the Mathematics Tripos and then Natural Sciences Part II in Physics.

This opportunity to study at the University of Cambridge must have excited him in the knowledge that he would become involved with the world's leading institution in the study of nuclear physics. In the 1920s, the Cavendish Laboratory at the University was instrumental in major discoveries surrounding the nucleus of the atom. Ernest Rutherford became its Director in 1919. He had seen the possibilities in revealing the characteristics of the atom, if, it could be bombarded by particles and monitored in some way. He was energetic, hard working, and, tellingly for Cambridge, a talent spotter of promising nuclear physicists who he attracted to his laboratory. In turn, he was held in high esteem and affection by them.

Those who worked at the Cavendish in the twenties and thirties achieved ground breaking discoveries in nuclear physics and were at the pinnacle of their subject. James Chadwick discovered the neutron. Mark Oliphant worked on the fusion reaction which was the basis of fusion powered nuclear reactors and the hydrogen bomb. Patrick Blackett made initial studies on cosmic radiation. J.D. Bernal began to define chemical structure using X-ray crystallography. Cockcroft and Walton demonstrably changed the nitrogen atom into another element by bombarding it with protons, sometimes referred to as splitting the atom. Edward Appleton studied the ionosphere and went on to perfect radar. This list of distinguished Cavendish Laboratory workers is not exhaustive and many of those who worked there received the ultimate accolade of the Nobel Prize. The Cavendish Laboratory was able to boast twelve Nobel Prize winners between 1904–1947.

This was the of learning atmosphere to which Alan Nunn May would be exposed.

Cambridge University has always attracted some of the most talented, cleverest, and erudite students into all its faculties, not just Physics. The university also provided its students with an opportunity to enjoy an active social life outside the requirement for serious study. It is considered quite normal, even expected, that students should ask questions and have their beliefs challenged. Debate and protests are vehement, usually in opposition to the current social and political climate. In the early thirties there was plenty to get angry about ; unemployment remained a desperate problem, social injustice, industrial strife and poverty were a part of life for the working classes. Wartime success had failed to guarantee economic stability. The emergence of the Labour Party, when they formed governments, in 1924 and 1929, was a much hoped for fresh start but it ebbed away. In 1931, Britain was in a state of economic collapse, it had abandoned its adherence to the gold standard and Ramsey McDonald formed a National Government in an attempt to bolster the country's fortunes. But it had failed to bring about a new beginning. It seemed that government prevaricated and postulated, but didn't make decisions. They were still living on past glories from the Victorian age, unable to furnish new ideas and drifting from one crisis to another. It was perhaps not surprising that there were those who for a signpost to the future turned their attention elsewhere. It seemed to many students and professors alike, that the future lay in the example set by the Marxist state adopted, post revolution, by the Russians. The Workers State, as it was sometimes referred to, appeared to be making encouraging strides, having disposed of capitalism and adopted a new belief in the sharing of wealth among its citizens, and the breaking down of class barriers. The Soviets' introduction of the Five Year Plan in 1929, had increased admiration for Russia's political stance. In the face of the inept government in Britain, the adoption of Marxist principles promised a better way forward.

Such principles were adopted by many artists, writers, philosophers and scientists. It became a cause to be celebrated by liberal professors and some became open and effusive in their beliefs. The University of Cambridge played a prominent part in the movement and those who espoused such beliefs, whilst in the minority, were listened to. Most were clever, talented individuals, with engaging personalities, often charming, and they attracted both the attention and admiration of others. They often held views which ran counter to university policies, which were thought to be out of touch with current thinking. Such views were frequently voiced at the numerous dining clubs which were usually selective in their membership and thus even more appealing to those who felt they were left out of the scheme of things. If you were not a Marxist, then you must be fascist, a far worse accusation to defend. Some were treated roughly by their political opponents; being thrown into the River Cam was not infrequent. This forum of Marxist believers included a number of luminaries; Maurice Dobb, academic economist; John Strachey, a Labour MP, writer and lecturer; Raymond Postgate, social historian and journalist and J.D. Bernal, an eminent scientist. Marxist ideology found favour in both the arts and science and brought together individuals from unexpected quarters.

One particular dining group, The Apostles, had been formed one hundred years previously by Alfred Tennyson in association with John Sterling and John Kemble. In the thirties it was hijacked by Marxist sympathisers, including Donald Maclean, Guy Burgess, Kim Philby and Anthony Blunt, the latter thought by many to be a scholar of outstanding ability and intellectually brilliant. They were to develop a close knit group, espousing communist ideals with a loyalty which was first and foremost towards its membership. To be seen as part of such a group meant you were a progressive thinker and challenged the unsatisfactory status quo. It seemed Marxism was a cause to be espoused and perhaps Alan Nunn May, who was not an Apostle, thought so too.

This was not an open admission of membership, or a relationship with the Communist Party. The idea of encouraging high minded undergraduates and academics to join the Communist Party, in particular those likely to obtain a place on the establishment ladder, has been attributed to Maxim Litvinov, the Russian envoy to London in 1929. He pursued his objectives gradually, quietly enmeshing selected individuals to the communist cause. He surmised that they would be loyal to one another, and would therefore not betray their Communist principles.

During the Easter Vacation of 1932, delegates from the Universities of Oxford and Cambridge, the London School of Economics and University College London, met at James Klugman's parents' house in Southwick Street, Hampstead, London. There they discussed tactics and future methods of collaboration with representatives from Communist Party Headquarters. Amongst those present was Douglas Frank Springhall, a founder member and national organiser. He and Clemens Palme Dutt were instrumental in the formation of the first communist cell at Cambridge University. They were to keep an eye out for promising talent which could be recruited to the Party. As regards recruitment as agents, i.e. spies, this was to remain in firm control of Russian hands. It was not for example, to be delegated to university dons, who were thought not to be competent in such matters.

By this time Alan Nunn May had been attracted to Marxist philosophy but was disinclined to spend too much time at meetings lest it have an affect on his chosen goal of a career in Physics.

By 1933, he had gained a First Class Honours in Part 1 of the Mathematics (Physics) Tripos and Part II of the Natural Science (Physics) Tripos. He went on to complete a Ph.D. *The Disintegration Of The Light Element by Alpha Particles*, via the Cavendish Laboratory at Cambridge in 1936. This latter work required a great deal of repetitive experimental work, much of which was boring. It was important that it be completed satisfactorily since this would be the minimum requirement for a top job in Physics. His initial supervisor had been James Chadwick who was replaced by Charles Ellis. On completion of the thesis he was examined by Ernest Rutherford. Although his experimental work was at times tedious, he was able to take considerable advantage of being in close contact at the Cavendish with luminaries such as John Cockcroft, Patrick Blackett and Mark Oliphant, not forgetting distinguished visitors including Einstein and Paul Dirac.

It was around this time that he joined the Communist Party and was considered by colleagues at the university to be a somewhat shy and introverted individual.

Files at the National Archives show that Alan visited Russia in 1936 and 1938. This was not unusual. Bernard Shaw; novelist, Professor Julian Huxley; scientist, and Lady Astor were amongst many high minded and distinguished individuals who visited Russia in the thirties and were overwhelmed and impressed with what they observed. Surely, they could not be wrong? Not everyone was convinced, and some trade union officials were sceptical about the claims being advanced. Visitors to Russia were carefully supervised and those who visited the country had to support the travel costs themselves, something which could not be undertaken by the working classes. Presumably Alan Nunn May received financial support of some form, as he had only recently completed his university studies.

He became a member of a trade union, The Association of Scientific Workers (AScW) and attended their meetings. An early note in MI5 files, states that he attended a Communist Party faction meeting of the AScW on Saturday 12 February 1938 at the Westmoreland Arms, George St., London.

After completion of his Ph.D., his supervisor Charles Ellis appointed him to a junior lectureship at King's College, London. The Physics Department had former distinguished heads such as Clerk Maxwell and Edward Appleton. Alan Nunn May commenced research into the detection of small amounts of radiation whilst at the same time preparing and delivering a three year physics syllabus for students.

In 1939 with the approach of war he joined a radar training scheme on the east coast. Soon King's College was evacuated from London to Bristol, and he had to leave his radar work to rejoin them there. He wanted to follow up on previous work, done in London, but much to his disappointment was dissuaded from doing so.

Eventually Cecil Powell invited him to join his team at Bristol who were developing photographic means for the detection of fast track particles in radioactive material. Bristol had a very modern and well equipped Physics Department but the work also necessitated close collaboration with Liverpool and the requirement of hundreds of measurements. In 1940 there began the frightening realisation that an atomic bomb might become a reality. Powell and Nunn May were to co-operate on experiments related to the theories being propounded by Chadwick, Peierls, Frisch, Oliphant and others. Nunn May even produced a model Geiger counter for measuring traces of radioactiviy. It was to be a fruitful period of work with Powell, whom he came to know on a personal level and admired and respected.

CHAPTER TWO

In 1942 at the suggestion of James Chadwick, Nunn May was asked by Sir Edward Appleton, Secretary to the Department of Science and Industrial Research (DSIR), to join a team at the Cavendish Laboratory which was engaged on the secret "Tube Alloys Project" headed by Dr H.H. Halban. This appointment was to be a major influence on the rest of his life.

The importance of this project can be traced back to scientific work undertaken in France during 1939. As a result of experiments conducted in Germany by Hahn, Meitner and Straussman on the effects of bombarding Uranium by neutrons, physicists began to investigate the possibilities of ensuing chain reactions and their likely outcome. Prominent amongst the teams searching for explanations were Fermi and Szilard at Columbia University in the USA, and Frederic Joliot-Curie, Hans von Halban, Lew Kowarski, and Francis Perrin at the College de France. Kowarski was Russian and Halban was Austrian but both had adopted French citizenship.

The French group began to make significant progress at working out the details of these complex reactions and the real possibility that they provided a significant release of energy which might be harnessed for peaceful purposes, but more sombrely, it indicated the real possibility of a new type of explosive device. In the race to further their knowledge, the French team held a significant advantage over the Americans in that they were able to purchase large amounts of uranium via a mining company, Union Miniere du Haut-Katanga in the Belgian Congo.

As a consequence of expanding their knowledge of these complex processes, it became necessary to acquire a moderator termed 'heavy water', which was available as a by-product of a hydroelectric scheme in Norway. By this time, war had been declared with Germany which was seeking to purchase heavy water from Norway. The Norwegians declined and in a top secret exercise, their entire stock of 185 kilos was smuggled to France. A month later, Germany declared war on Norway. The Germans were also advancing swiftly towards France and Raoul Dautry, French Minister of Armaments ordered Joliot-Curie, Halban and Kowarski to leave for England. Joliot-Curie chose to remain in France, and on 18 June 1940, Halban and Kowarski left Bordeaux with twenty six cans of heavy water for England. They were welcomed by James Chadwick and John Cockcroft who, aware of their work, invited them to continue their experiments at the Cavendish Laboratory, in Cambridge, alongside other nuclear physicists.

At the same time the British were also studying these same nuclear reactions. Two exiled German scientists, Rudolf Peierls and Otto Frisch had shown that if Uranium 235 (0.7%) could be separated from the Uranium 238 (99.3%) in natural uranium, an atomic bomb could be produced with no requirement for a moderator.

These developments persuaded the British to coordinate this volume of expanding knowledge via a group called the MAUD Committee formed in April 1940. Its membership included George Paget Thomson, Chairman; Patrick Blackett, James Chadwick, Mark Oliphant, John Cockcroft and Philip Moon. All of whom were leading experts in nuclear physics. Chadwick, Cockcroft, Blackett, and Thomson were or were to become Nobel Prize winners. In September 1940, a delegation was sent to North America to exchange scientific information and they were able to report back on the atomic research being conducted in the USA and Canada. They also took the opportunity to explore the possibility of relocating their researchers to the USA, away from German bombing.

During 1940, a further scientific breakthrough at the Cavendish Laboratory occurred with the discovery of Plutonium 239 resulting from the bombardment of uranium. Plutonium 239 had similar properties to Uranium 235. It was fissionable and could easily be separated from uranium. As regards the production of an atomic bomb the issue of a moderator could be bypassed. The work of Halban and Kowarski and the pursuit of plutonium as a component for an atomic device could not be done at Cambridge because of inadequate resources and it was left to the Americans to follow this line of research. This work was independently confirmed in the USA at the University of Berkeley. By July 1941, the MAUD Committee had produced two reports; *The Use of Uranium as a Source of Power*, and *The Use of Uranium for a Bomb*. Winston Churchill appointed Sir John Anderson, formerly a physical chemist, and Lord President of the Council, to be responsible for a British nuclear programme.

The Defence Services Panel of the government's Scientific Advisory Committee having received the reports from the MAUD Committee, recommended that work on the atomic bomb should be given the highest national importance. The reports were sent to the USA where, surprisingly, they elicited little response. Mark Oliphant then flew to the USA and discovered that the reports had been kept in a locked safe and had not been circulated to the appropriate scientists. Oliphant contacted Ernest Lawrence, James Conant, Enrico Fermi and Arthur Conant and persuaded them of the need for urgent action. The Americans now realised that an atomic bomb was feasible and galvanised their resources. A deputation visited the UK in November 1941 in this spirit of collaboration, but the offer was not taken up.

Later, in 1941, the nuclear programme became too large for the MAUD Committee to manage. A new organisation known, for security reasons, as the Directorate of Tube Alloys was set up in the DSIR with Wallace Akers as Chief Executive, responsible to Sir Edward Appleton for administrative matters, and to Sir John Anderson, Lord President of the Council, for matters of policy. Its headquarters were on the fourth floor of Shell Mex House, The Strand, London WC2. It's remit was to conduct the whole of the British nuclear programme.

By 1942, the Americans had confirmed the importance of plutonium as a source of an atomic bomb. Their experimental work was shown to be more thorough than that of Halban and Kowarski, and was not just valuable in terms of post war value nuclear power but as part of the construction of an atomic bomb. This only became apparent when in 1942, Akers led a mission to the USA to persuade them to accept the Cambridge team, including Halban and Kowarski, to work as an independent unit at the University of Chicago where Arthur Compton was leading the effort to isolate and extract plutonium. They declined, saying that they would have to be part of the American effort. The mission were astounded by the speed at which the Americans were developing their nuclear programme and the atomic bomb project. In June 1942, the United States Army under General Grove took over all aspects of process development, engineering design, procurement of materials and site selection. Grove also instituted a security clampdown. All cooperation and collaboration with the scientists in the UK ceased. This was both a bitter disappointment and a major irritation to them. It was doubly irritating since their work on slow neutron research, not considered relevant to the atomic bomb, could provide a route to the production of plutonium, although confirmation of this had only just been received by the Cavendish group.

In 1942 the pressure to pursue nuclear research at the Cavendish Laboratory was intense, with Halban and Kowarski leading the way. It was agreed between Appleton and Chadwick that a British physicist be added to the team since it was largely composed of refugees from war torn Europe. Chadwick put forward Alan Nunn May. In their discussions regarding the job to be done, Chadwick appears to have made an indirect remark about the political leanings of those involved. Chadwick was well aware of the Marxist leanings of other scientists involved but felt that, provided Nunn May adopted a discreet approach there should not be a problem. Such was the desperate need to obtain top physicists to do the work that their political affiliations were considered a side issue. Nunn May was sorry to leave Bristol but significant pressure was brought to bear on him, emphasising that this job was of the highest national importance. He must have been delighted at the prospect of working with so many distinguished physicists even though it was evident that the working practises and awkward personality of some of them, might cause him problems. At the time he was still engaged as a lecturer at King's College and was working in Bristol. There was an urgency among those engaged on the Tube Alloys Project and he was allowed a special dispensation to continue his duties as an examiner at King's College. All of these arrangements required the agreement of Professor Sir Lawrence Bragg who was Head of the Cavendish Laboratory. Nunn May's place of work would be at the Cavendish Laboratory and his salary (£500 per annum) would be funded by the DSIR.

At his interview Nunn May sought assistance in finding accommodation in Cambridge, which was proving difficult. They would do what they could. Eventually he went to live at 16, Jesus Lane, Cambridge. His references were not taken up, since they had considerable scientific knowledge of him already. He was sent an application form for employment by the DSIR which he duly signed.

The terms of his employment by the DSIR indicate the groundbreaking and top secret nature of the work and had been carefully drafted with the benefit of legal advice. They are set out below.

> I, Alan Nunn May understand that the investigation on Tube Alloys Research or any work in connection therewith on which I am engaged at the Cavendish Laboratory, Cambridge is being undertaken on behalf of the Department of Scientific and Industrial Research, that it is confidential and no information concerning it is to be communicated or published in any way by me except (a) to those of my colleagues of whose names I have been or will from time to time be informed in writing by Dr H.H. Halban or (b) to the Secretary of the Department or (c) to the Director of Tube Alloys Research of the Department or (d) to a person who shall have been notified in writing to me by Dr R.H. Halban or by the Secretary or Director, as aforesaid as authorised to receive such information.
>
> I have seen and read copies of the Official Secrets Act, 1911, 1920 and 1939.
>
> I understand that the results of the investigation, (hereinafter called "the results" which expression includes as well as all principal discoveries inventions and other results arising from the investigation all discoveries inventions and other results arising from the investigation which are indirectly concerned with its principal objects)

are the property solely of the Department and in consideration of the Department entrusting me with the investigation or with any work in connection therewith I undertake not to make any application for any patent or other protection in respect of any discoveries or inventions without the prior written consent of the Department, and if and when and only when, called upon to do by the Department through its representative duly authorised in manner as stated at paragraph (d) above, to sign any document and to do any other act or thing at the Department's expense, as may be necessary to secure to the Department or its nominee any Letters Patent or other protection or rights in the results and to assign any such Letters Patent or other protection or rights as shall be directed by the Department; but this shall not prevent me, if I so desire, from applying to the Department for an ex gratia award in respect of any such discovery or invention.

I understand that the use of the results will be controlled, and all negotiations for such use conducted by the Department and in consideration as aforesaid I undertake to do nothing in relation to the results or any Letters Patent or other protection or rights which may arise, therefore or obtain in connection therewith except with the prior written consent of, or by the prior written direction of, the Department, and only in accordance with such consent or direction.

I understand that these provisions apply also to any other investigations forming part of the same general programme on which I may have been engaged in the past or may be engaged in the future on behalf of any Department of H.M. Government in so far as these are not covered by any other written agreement or statement past or future signed by me.

Dated 29th day May 1942

Signed *Alan Nunn May* and witnessed by *H.F. Freundlich*

The scale and resources required to pursue nuclear research were enormous. Also the pursuit of certain objectives in a short time period were demanding. The United Kingdom was already heavily committed to the war effort and in order for the project to continue, it was necessary that the leading scientists be transferred to America.

The Americans had already rejected this on grounds of security in that certain members of the British group were refugees from countries occupied by Germany such as France, Austria and Czechoslovakia. It was thought they might be compromised by their families being under an occupied power.

It was under these circumstances that Alan Nunn May joined up with the Cavendish Laboratory following Chadwick's request. He would not have been aware of much of the background to his appointment and it was difficult for him to catch up with the work which had been undertaken. Complex science was being undertaken by different nationalities in two different countries and the pressure to make progress was enormous. Already certain key scientific information had been withheld from the Cavendish group and it became apparent to Nunn May that Halban was a very difficult person to work with. Halban had produced many noteworthy scientific papers and had worked in eminent laboratories, but he took an autocratic stance with colleagues and this hierarchical approach was rebuffed by the Americans. They did not want him and his colleagues as part of their team. Therefore the logical conclusion of combining the talents working in the USA with scientists from the UK was rejected by them.

Meanwhile Nunn May set out on a programme of experimental work at the Cavendish Laboratory alongside other physicists and chemists. During this time he was to spend considerable effort in investigating the likely effects of a bomb dropped by the Germans in order to spread radioactive contamination. There was considerable anxiety that they were active in this field and Nunn May wrote several scientific reports on the likely outcome. Thankfully the rumours of a dirty bomb eventually came to nothing.

Behind the scenes, following the American rejection of the British approach to join their scientific teams, an alternative proposal was agreed, that a joint British Canadian effort be established in Canada leading to the production of plutonium. This arrangement was accepted by the Americans and they agreed to exchange information relating to the design of the plant.

Not everybody was in agreement with the proposal and some were sceptical about the outcome and in particular had no wish to serve under Halban. Nevertheless, pressure was applied to all of the Cavendish team that this move to Canada was essential for winning the war against Germany. Kowarski chose to remain in the UK.

Thus within six months of his appointment at the Cavendish, Nunn May was informed that arrangements were in hand for the research team to be transferred to a laboratory in Montreal, Canada, in collaboration with the National Research Council of Canada. The research team would continue to be a section of the Directorate of Tube Alloys, but he would now be employed directly by the latter.

The appointment could be terminated by either side subject to restrictions imposed by Defence Regulations. The previous conditions placed upon him whilst he was employed at the Cavendish Laboratory remained in place, including his obligations under the Official Secrets Act.

His salary would continue to be £500 per annum plus Civil Service War Bonus of £19, 1s per annum. While in Canada he would receive an allowance granted to all U.K. government civilian personnel working in Canada. This was £6.30d per day for the first month and £5.40d per day thereafter.

He discussed the move at an interview with Sir Edward Appleton on 23 December 1942, and confirmed his acceptance in writing on 28 December 1942.

During this busy period at Cambridge, Alan Nunn May became reacquainted with political friends who urged him to become more active in Communist Party activities. Alan reminded them that he had signed the Official Secrets Act, but was told that other colleagues had done the same, and in any case the whole object was to win the war against Germany. He went on to attend weekly meetings. Prior to the request that he should join the team in Canada he approached the Chairman of his Communist Party group to discuss his doubts about leaving to be part of such a venture. The transfer to Canada was widely known amongst the scientific community and he was asked if any of this information was known to the Russians who were allies. Alan did not know but agreed to meet a representative from the Russian embassy.

A meeting was set up and Alan met up with a person in a London café and handed over a brief description of the current stage of the project and what, as far as he knew, was planned for the future. What at the outset seemed to be an innocuous exercise turned out to be an unsettling meeting. The general atmosphere he found disturbing. He got the distinct impression that he was being observed in the café. This was to be the first fateful step along the road to his entrapment.

Alan returned to Cambridge and reported to his party group leader. He was told that while the information he had provided was interesting it was not that important. Such information would be forthcoming from various sources and in any case these would only be issues at the end of the war.

This was a standard tactic employed by Russian intelligence to downplay information, but it was a carefully worked out method to prepare the way for access to further information. His party group leader emphasised that he must go to Canada and support the war effort. Whilst there he should obtain a flat from which he could gather and supply information. Alan protested but was told vehemently that this would demonstrate clearly his support for the Russian efforts in pursuit of the war. In any case who would suspect anything so bold in such a top secret undertaking? He agreed to comply and was informed that arrangements would take place once he was in Canada for a prearranged contact with a stranger from Montreal. That contact would use the code phrase "Greetings from Alex". If he was beginning to be alarmed, the next instructions were even more threatening. On no account must he have anything to do with other approaches that came via any other route. There were many left wing factions in Canada and he must not get involved with any of them. Not long after this Alan was to meet up with Douglas Springhall, Secretary of the Communist Party in a café in London. When Springhall asked Alan whether he was making arrangements to send information to the Russians while in Canada he obeyed orders and denied all knowledge of such a thing. Receiving such a response, perhaps Springhall knew that the trap was set.

CHAPTER THREE

On 16 January 1943, Nunn May embarked at Swansea for the voyage to Halifax, Nova Scotia, Canada to work on the secret Tube Alloys Atomic Energy Project at Montreal.

The Montreal Laboratory had been established by the National Research Council of Canada to undertake nuclear research and to take over some of the scientists and projects from the Tube Alloys nuclear project in the U.K. It was top secret and the scientists involved were not permitted to discuss their work with anyone, not even scientists in other fields. The work was associated with the harnessing of nuclear power for peaceful purposes, and was not concerned with the manufacture of the atomic bomb. Initially they occupied an old house at 3740 Simpson Street belonging to McGill University but eventually moved into a new building originally intended as a medical school, but which, through lack of funds, had never been fitted out. The Director of the laboratory, which had about 300 staff, was Hans Halban formerly of the Cavendish Laboratory.

In order to carry out their work, the Montreal team depended on the USA for supplies of heavy water from its plant at Trail in British Columbia. They attached conditions to this arrangement, principally that the Montreal laboratory should direct its research on lines suggested by Du Pont. They also placed further restrictions on the exchange of scientific information on account of their concerns regarding the varied nationalities of the Montreal team.

On his arrival in Canada, it fell to Nunn May to discuss the project with physicists from North America and also the work already accomplished by Halban. His hosts were sceptical about Halban's work (as was Alan) and also their knowledge of the subject was far in advance of his own. The project was proving very difficult to get off the ground and although the laboratory was being fitted out there was still no meaningful communication with the Americans. It had been anticipated that the Montreal Laboratory would be able to avail itself of the resources being developed at the Chicago laboratory, but the American security clampdown prevented this from happening. Alan joined the Experimental Physics section headed by Pierre Auger while Chemistry was under F.A. Paneth, a radiochemist.

Meantime the project stalled. As well as scientific disputes with the Americans there was also mounting political friction concerning who would control the atomic bomb. Scientific meetings between the Canadian and American groups did take place in Chicago and from some of the unofficial information available, the Canadian group were able to make limited progress. After a protracted period the Canadian group were eventually able to prove conclusively that Halban's work on heavy water in Cambridge was correct.

The choice of Halban as Director of the Laboratory was to prove unsatisfactory. It appeared that he was unreasonable in his demands of administrative staff and was also found to be both impetuous and slow to react. He did not communicate well with the National Research Council of Canada.

At the Quebec Conference in August 1943, the unsatisfactory state of affairs between the American and Canadian teams was discussed by Winston Churchill and President Roosevelt. They re-emphasised the need for close collaboration between the two countries, but this appeared to have no observable effect. There was low morale and in 1943, the Canadian Government came close to cancelling the project. Eventually through the combined efforts of James Chadwick, the British scientist, and General Groves, Head of the American Nuclear Project and Dr C.J. Mackenzie, President of the National Research Council of Canada, good sense prevailed and the project was saved.

In April 1944, the United States agreed that Canada should build a nuclear reactor for the production of plutonium. The USA now fully supported the reactor project and supplied uranium and heavy water. An expanding knowledge of nuclear physics continued to throw up other options regarding nuclear power and also the production of an atomic bomb. It now became possible to test these findings at the major facility in Chicago. This was to be vital in the building of the first nuclear reactor in Canada. The sheer scope and scale of the work cannot be underestimated. Not only were there significant problems to be resolved, in the understanding of nuclear physics, but a host of other problems had to be solved. They included the development of measuring devices, increased measures regarding radiation safety, and the never before undertaken, engineering of a nuclear plant. Things improved after the Quebec Conference but not quickly enough for the Canadian team. They still required information from the Americans which they were reluctant to provide. When Alan Nunn May had the distinction of being asked to go to Chicago and commence experiments in their atomic pile, he was asked by his fellow scientists to bring back answers to many of their queries. Whilst in Chicago, Herbert Anderson, who was in charge of atomic pile experiments, agreed to make available some of the reports in order to help out the Canadian team. Alan conducted his experiments and then made copious notes copied from these reports in answer to requests from his colleagues. It was a laborious process but invaluable to them.

John Cockcroft replaced Halban as the new Director of the Montreal Laboratory and arrived on 26 April 1944. Under Cockcroft, morale improved considerably and a sense of purpose was restored. Kowarski joined the project as he had declined to work under Halban. Halban was to leave in March 1945. Nunn May was a senior member of the Nuclear Physics Division and as such had knowledge of all the Physics work and was in consultation with others to resolve problems related to atomic energy. He was a member of the Atomic Pile Design Committee and the Metal Production Committee. The Atomic Pile is used to produce Plutonium and provide a source of neutrons for investigation into problems of nuclear physics. He also liaised with the Canadians and with workers in the U.K. regarding the latest ideas for the production and fabrication of uranium. The aim was to build a nuclear reactor in Canada as a source of power for peaceful purposes. This was a major task bringing with it a considerable cost. Alan Nunn May was to play a significant role in experiments to test whether the nuclear physics theories being explored would work in a reactor. He was to propose building a pilot plant to test these theories which would not involve vast expenditure. There were ongoing safety concerns which also needed to be addressed. This meant Alan needed to visit Chicago frequently in order to pursue the work. A part of his experimental work involved comparing the properties of Uranium 233 and Uranium 235 and determining whether they were suitable for bomb making or the harnessing of nuclear power. The work was done in conjunction with Herbert Anderson in Chicago and on its completion the samples of each isotope were divided. The Chicago group kept one half and Alan was given the other half. This was considered good experimental practice in that any future verification of the work could be undertaken on the original samples.

In 1944, the Chalk River Laboratories, located near Ottawa, were opened, and by September 1945 they operated the first nuclear reactor outside of the United States. Meanwhile Nunn May continued his work in Montreal through 1945 supporting the nuclear programme. Nunn May's scientific work was successful and he was also to receive word that his application for a Readership at King's College, London, to commence in October 1945, had been successful. He would also be Acting Head of Department in the absence of Charles Ellis. His academic future was assured.

During this period rumours that the Americans were building an atomic bomb were rife in the scientific community. In July 1945 the Americans completed a nuclear test in New Mexico. It became clear that this knowledge was to be kept secret from all the major allies including Russia. Bits and pieces of news filtered out slowly amongst scientists. A number had their doubts as to if, or how, the device would be used and what the post-war consequences would be. Alan Nunn May was among them and because of his political sympathy for the Russians, he felt that it was surely wrong that they were being left out of any dialogue. His political doctrine was about to be tested and, the Russians, as they had promised, made contact with him. Veiled hints of the interest in scientific work in America and Canada were to become both demanding and menacing.

Having fulfilled its objective, the Montreal laboratory was eventually closed in 1946 and its resources merged with Chalk River.

In September 1945, Nunn May's employment in the Tube Alloys Project ceased and on 17 September 1945 he flew back to the United Kingdom by RAF transport. He arrived at Prestwick Airport at 6:15 a.m. There was nobody to welcome him back. However an MI5 officer discreetly observed his arrival and began to follow him. The presence of such a person was a result of sensational events that had arisen twelve days before Nunn May's departure from Canada.

CHAPTER FOUR

On the evening of 5 September 1945, Igor Gouzenko, who had been a cipher clerk at the Soviet Embassy in Ottawa for two years, left for home taking with him a number of secret files.

It is worth elaborating on Gouzenko's status in the Embassy in order to explain the importance of the documentation to which he had access. Igor Gouzenko was twenty six years old and had been selected, at the Moscow Engineering Academy by the NKVD (forerunner of the KGB), to be trained in intelligence and cipher work. He was posted to the Red Army military intelligence school in Moscow and ultimately conscripted into the GRU, the intelligence section of the Red Army which was responsible for the collection of foreign military and scientific intelligence. He gained a commission in the army and saw service against Nazi Germany. After his war service, he was posted to the Soviet Legation in Ottawa in June 1943. His wife joined him and they rented an apartment at 511 Somerset Street, Ottawa. The Russian Embassy was located at 285 Charlotte Street, Ottawa. His office was located on the second floor.

His job for the GRU (Soviet Military Intelligence), was to encipher and decipher messages sent between the military attaché and the Director of Military Intelligence in Moscow. The internal organisation of the embassy ensured that separate sections, including the GRU, were independent of one another. They did not communicate with each other. Even the ambassador did not know of the activities of the separate sections. The Head of the GRU was a Colonel Zabotin.

His office was at a separate address in Range Road. Equipment was installed at this address for copying sensitive documents prior to their being transmitted to Moscow.

It was the policy for cipher clerks to be recalled to Moscow after twelve months but because of his special work this was deferred, as a result of a plea made by his boss Colonel Zabotin. Eventually in August 1945, he was ordered to return to Moscow. By now Gouzenko was enjoying life in Canada and was perturbed by the future loss of his freedom. In particular he disliked the fact that Soviet intelligence was undermining Canadian institutions and a government who had helped Russia during the war. He knew that the files he took with him would uncover Russian espionage at a high level in Canada. Their disclosure was to create alarm in the intelligence services of the western alliance who had been engaged in the war against Germany.

Initially he took the files to a newspaper, the Ottawa Journal, rather than the police, because his experience of the Russian police had taught him to be suspicious of their motives. On his first visit, that evening, to the newspaper, he became anxious that the newspaper might have spies on its payroll and returned home to his wife, Svetlana. She urged him to return to the newspaper office, although it was late evening, and try again.

When he returned, the editor of the newspaper had gone home, but he managed to show some of the files (they were all written in Russian), to a member of staff and explained who he was and where he worked. He was told that they couldn't help him with that kind of thing and that he should go to the Royal Canadian Mounted Police (RCMP).

By then, he was becoming increasingly desperate, and decided to go to the Minister of Justice's offices. By this time it was almost midnight, and he was met by a man in RCMP uniform who said that he would have to return the next day. The following day he did not return to the Soviet Embassy but toured government offices in Ottawa, where again his story was not believed. He even went back to the same newspaper office but was met with the same lack of interest.

He returned to his apartment, by which time the staff at the Soviet Embassy must have been concerned at his absence. Later that evening he heard a knock at the door of his apartment. The caller hearing a noise inside, called out in Russian. Gouzenko recognising the voice of one of the embassy chauffeurs, remained silent. When the man went away, Gouzenko made contact with Harold Main, a neighbour, who fortuitously was a Sergeant in the Royal Canadian Air Force and explained to him his situation. Meantime Gouzenko's wife had explained their dilemma to the occupant of the apartment directly opposite, a Mrs Elliott. She offered Gouzenko, his wife and son, shelter for the night since her husband and children were away.

Sergeant Main went to the police, and two officers came and questioned Gouzenko at Mrs Elliott's flat. Towards midnight, Sergeant Main was disturbed by four men banging on the door of Gouzenko's flat. He told them that the Gouzenkos' were away. They left briefly but returned later and were observed breaking into Gouzenko's flat. The police, who were by now alerted to the situation, were called, and on their arrival discovered four men ransacking Gouzenko's flat.

The police questioned the interlopers, who said they had permission to enter the flat since their colleague was away and they needed important papers which were in the apartment. They showed their papers to the police and in the general disturbance were allowed to leave the scene.

With the Canadian Police now alerted, Gouzenko was secretly taken into custody on 6 September and his documents handed over. On 8 September the Canadian Department for External Affairs received a note from the Soviet Embassy explaining the break in at Gouzenko's flat. The embassy said that Gouzenko had stolen money from them and that the Canadian authorities should take all measures to arrest him, and that he should be deported to Russia.

Gouzenko and his family subsequently received protection for many months and were kept at a secret location. In the years following they were under constant protection, provided with new identification, and resettled by the Canadian authorities.

The documents Gouzenko had taken from the Russian Embassy revealed to the Canadian authorities and, eventually, the rest of the world, the extent of the organisation and apparatus of the Soviet intelligence network. Up to this point, everyone had considered Russia an ally in the war against Germany and not a threat to the western alliance.

On examination the files Gouzenko had removed proved to contain detailed information about a Russian spy network which had infiltrated military and political personnel in Canada at the highest level. They had penetrated the Department of External Affairs, National Research Council, Department of National Defence and the office of the High Commissioner. It implicated about eighteen people including Fred Rose, a member of the Canadian Parliament, Dr Raymond Boyer Assistant Professor of Chemistry at McGill University, and Captain Gordon Lunan of the Canadian Army.

When it became clear as to the seriousness of the intelligence leakage, a meeting of the Privy Council took place at Government House in Ottawa on 6 October 1945. The Governor General, on the recommendation of the acting Prime Minister, J.L. Ilsley, took legal steps to allow the interrogation, detention of persons and the entry into premises in Canada where there was reasonable suspicion of secret and confidential information being communicated to a foreign power.

The revelations were not confined to Canadians, since the documents stolen by Gouzenko also revealed that a major informer was a citizen of the United Kingdom, called Alan Nunn May. The information was detailed and very specific, and included transcripts of messages relayed to Moscow concerning Nunn May (codename Alek), as well as arrangements for him to rendezvous with contacts once he had returned to England. Gouzenko's stolen documents gave evidence of an extensive collaboration between Nunn May and Colonel Zabotin, Military Attache at the Russian Embassy and the operator of an espionage system in Canada. According to Gouzenko, Nunn May had been in the pay of the Soviets for many years and was a secret member of the Communist Party of Great Britain. As regards his membership of the Communist Party, this would have been no surprise to his colleagues since they also had similar leanings.

CHAPTER FIVE

Nunn May had arrived in Canada in January 1943, and after a lapse of about a year, Colonel Zabotin at the Russian Embassy was ordered by Moscow to make contact with him via Fred Rose a member of the Canadian Parliament and a member of the Communist Party. Zabotin would not use Rose but thought it preferable to use an assistant, Lieutenant Pavel Angelov (code name Baxter). Moscow assigned the cover name Alek to Nunn May and a password, "best regards from Mikel". It was therefore assumed by intelligence, at that time, that Nunn May had been briefed before leaving England and told to await a contact.

At a series of meetings with Angelov, Nunn May gave him nuclear data concerning the use of plutonium and uranium and aspects related to the design of the American atomic pile and the difficulties they had encountered. This information was cabled to Moscow and a report in Nunn May's handwriting was sent by diplomatic bag.

At another meeting with Angelov, Nunn May provided him with a container labelled "250 ", now thought to be Uranium 235. This was disputed at the time but it was thought Nunn May might have obtained such material in Chicago. This was again sent to Moscow. Amongst the papers was a note which indicated that Zabotin had authorised Angelov to make Nunn May a payment of 200 dollars wrapped around a whisky bottle.

Nunn May also provided scientific details of the detonation of the first atomic device at Los Alamos in New Mexico on 16 July 1945 and the atomic bomb dropped on Hiroshima on 6 August 1945. He also provided a sample of Uranium 233 and a report on electronically operated shells invented by the Americans for use against Japanese suicide pilots.

The following is one example of many telegrams Gouzenko removed from the Russian Embassy. This is a translation of a telegram sent from the Soviet Military Attache in Ottawa, Colonel Zabotin (code name Grant), to Moscow dated 9 July 1945.

> To The Director
> The Facts given by Alec:
> 1) The experiments with the atomic bomb were conducted in New Mexico (with "49", "94–239"). The bomb thrown on Japan was made uranium 235. It is known that the release of uranium 235 is produced to the amount of 400 grams daily at the magnetic separation plant in Clinton. The release of "49" is likely two times greater (some graphite units composed on 250 mega watts i.e. 250 grams a day). The scientific research work in this field is scheduled to be published, but without technical details. The Americans already have a printed book on the subject.
> 2) Alec handed over to us a plantinum with 162 micrograms of uranium 233 in the form of acid contained in a thin lamina. We had no news about the mail.
>
> *Grant*

Nunn May's major interest was clearly nuclear research, but he was also able to provide information about an electronic device the Americans were developing against Japanese suicide pilots. He could even give the technical details associated with it so he must have had contact with someone working in that field.

The breadth of the Russian involvement is further revealed by the activities of Norman Veal who worked in the Montreal laboratory alongside Nunn May. Veal had worked in the Meteorology Service of the Air Ministry in the UK during 1939, was a member of the

AScW and had been connected with the Hendon branch of young communists. He had openly discussed with Nunn May the possibility of handing over information about the atomic bomb. Nunn May demurred and reported Veal's approach. Apparently Veal discussed this in the presence of his wife which Nunn May thought careless. All this was reported to Zabotin who advised against any collaboration with Veal. This supports the initial instructions conveyed to Nunn May prior to his departure from the UK.

The Soviets expected that dialogue with Nunn May would continue once he had returned to the U.K. Once again papers removed by Gouzenko revealed telegrams dated 22 August 1945 from Moscow to Zabotin in Canada containing arrangements he should make with Nunn May to meet with a Soviet contact once he arrived back in London.

The meeting place was to be in front of the British Museum, on the opposite side of the street from Museum Street. Nunn May was instructed to arrive from the direction of Tottenham Court Road, while the contact would come from Southampton Row. The time was originally to be 23:00, but was altered by Moscow to 20:00, as it would then still be daylight.

Nunn May was to carry *The Times* under his left arm, whilst the contact man would carry the *Picture Post*.

The contact would ask the shortest way to the Strand, and Nunn May would reply:

'Well come along. I am going that way.' Nunn May would begin the conversation with his password 'Best regards from Mikel.' The suggested dates for a rendezvous were 7, 17 and 27 October 1945.

These revelations initiated frenetic activity from the intelligence services on both sides of the Atlantic. Nunn May was due to depart from Canada on 15 September, just nine days after Gouzenko had removed the files from the Russian Embassy, so there was little time to decide what should be done.

On 10 September 1945, a coded Top Secret message was sent from Malcolm MacDonald, Canadian Department for External Affairs via New York for the attention of Sir Alexander Cadogan, at the Foreign Office. It said that Alan Nunn May, an agent of Soviet Intelligence, had provided Colonel Zabotin with useful and valuable information on research developments, including samples of Uranium 235, which had been flown to Moscow. It alerted officials to the fact that Nunn May was due to fly back to the United Kingdom on 15 September and that there were detailed instructions as to how he should make contact with a Russian agent in London.

Also, on 10 September, the Canadians contacted Nunn May's boss in Canada, Dr Cockcroft, Head of the Montreal Research Laboratory. They requested from him an estimate as to how much of his knowledge Nunn May could have passed to others. His response described what information and materials Nunn May had access to. They included the role of Uranium 235 and 239 in Atomic Bombs. He also said that Nunn May had access to samples of Uranium 233, and might have obtained uranium metal irradiated in the atomic pile. Such samples would be of great value to Russia as they had no known uranium deposits.

Nunn May now acquired the code name of Primrose for use in all messages by MI5. The Canadian authorities needed to decide whether Nunn May should be allowed to return to the U.K. as he was due to fly home in less that a week. He might disappear or defect in the meantime and they did not wish to alert him. The Canadian and U.K. authorities decided that Nunn May should be allowed to return to the U.K., but that his movements should be carefully monitored on his arrival back in England.

More and more intelligence was acquired including whether the information in the papers stolen by Gouzenko was reliable. During this time the whereabouts of Gouzenko remained secret, in order to delay alerting Russian intelligence. Gouzenko's material was being examined by the intelligence services in London, via cipher messages and telegrams from the RCMP. In the few days leading up to Nunn May's departure for the U.K. there was secret contact with Canada and much debate about the reliability of the information, since London had not seen any of the original documents. There was also some doubt as to whether there was sufficient evidence to bring appropriate charges against Nunn May. Again there was concern that Nunn May should not have any inkling that he was being monitored, whilst they sought to gather further incriminating evidence. Canada and London closely synchronised their operations.

As Alan Nunn May made his arrangements to fly home on 16 September 1945, the RCMP and MI5 made their plans to monitor his journey and ensure that he was followed on arrival in the United Kingdom.

The RCMP arranged that their Detective Sergeant Bayfield would travel on the same flight, posing as a Mr Bayfield, a special courier for our High Commissioner in Canada. Bayfield would also be carrying documents to support the case against Nunn May. There was to be strictly no contact between them. Bayfield was to be given special assistance to travel from Prestwick to London with his documents without arousing any suspicion. He would be met by MI5 officers with the password, 'How do you like our lowlands weather', to which Bayfield would reply, 'I have not seen much of it yet but it is rather like our maritime provinces'.

Meanwhile Nunn May arranged for his excess luggage to be forwarded by sea on the SS Rideau Park. It was due to arrive at Avonmouth Docks, Bristol, on 24 September.

CHAPTER SIX

Nunn May flew back on RAF Transport Command and arrived at Prestwick Airport at 6:15 a.m. on Monday 17 September 1945. A member of MI5 discreetly observed his arrival and was able to identify him from a photograph. He was carrying a large suitcase, a brown leather travelling bag and a large dispatch case. After passing through Customs, he breakfasted alone and then made a long distance call. At about 1 p.m. Nunn May, along with ten other passengers including Bayfield and a member of MI5, flew to Blackbushe Airport arriving at 3:10 p.m. He then, along with four other passengers, travelled to Camberley Railway Station and boarded the 4:05 p.m. train to Waterloo. Nunn May then engaged a taxi with three other men and was driven away, followed by MI5.

The taxi made its way to Russell Square, where the other men were dropped off and Nunn May proceeded alone to the Dominion Hotel in Lancaster Gate. The following morning Tuesday 18 September he made his way to Holborn via the underground and then walked to Kings College in the Strand arriving at about 10:30 p.m. He stayed for lunch and at 2:40 p.m. went to the Aldwych branch of Barclay's Bank in the Strand. There he passed over a buff coloured form but did not appear to withdraw any money. He returned to Kings College and left at 4 p.m. with a male colleague to have tea in a nearby restaurant.

All of this monitoring was undertaken by MI5. They noted that nothing of special interest had occurred and they withdrew observation. MI5 were still very tentative about paying too much attention to Nunn

May. The intelligence services obtained permission to place a phone tap on various telephones which Nunn May would use. They were Paddington 6667, (Dominions Hotel, Lancaster Gate), and Temple Bar 5651, (Kings College in the Strand). Checks were also to be made on incoming and outgoing mail.

With the war in Europe not long over, and the still unrepaired bomb damage to property in London, accommodation was difficult to obtain. Nunn May made a number of calls with a view to finding a flat, and his mother wrote to him, that a Mr and Mrs Wyatt might be able to help him as they had recently vacated a flat, and he should contact Mr Wyatt, at Lloyds Bank Head Office in Lombard Street. Nunn May also telephoned scientific colleagues concerning future scientific meetings and the AScW and the War Office asking to speak to Charles Ellis its Scientific Adviser, formerly of King's College.

On 18 September, the day after Nunn May's return to the U.K., Captain Liddell of MI5 met with a Mr Ricketts who was deputising for Sir John Anderson, and Mr Roger Makins of the Foreign Office at the Cabinet Office. They discussed the issue of preventing Nunn May from seeing confidential information whilst not arousing his suspicion. They called in Wallace Akers, Director of Tube Alloys Research and outlined the revelations about Nunn May. Akers was shocked at what he heard. as he rated Nunn May highly as a physicist.

Arrangements were made to keep highly sensitive information from Nunn May although again, this was difficult since he could quite legitimately see reports from various sources as he wanted to remain active and get a job in atomic research. The decision to exclude him from sensitive atomic research needed to be handled with great care by Akers and Cockcroft. At that same meeting Makins raised the possibility of marking documents received by Nunn May to see if they turned up in Russian hands. Again every effort must be made to ensure Nunn May did not leave the country.

This latter concern was to result in instructions to London airfields to be vigilant about the take off or landing of any Russian aircraft and the movement of personnel therein. This was a result of information emanating yet again from Gouzenko, to the affect that somebody called Zasansky, who had raised suspicions whilst serving in the

Czechlosovak Embassy in Canada, had passed through London, at the time unnoticed, six months previously.

There still remained scepticism regarding any envisaged prosecution of Nunn May. The additional information brought from Canada began to make an impact on that decision. In a memorandum of 21 September, Marriott of MI5 had shown examples of Nunn May's handwriting in documents containing espionage information to Captain Jim Skardon of MI5. He was sure that it was Nunn May's handwriting.

On 21 September a further MI5 memorandum, reaffirmed the difficulties encountered in maintaining surveillance without raising Nunn May's suspicions. They knew from tapping his telephone that he would soon be leaving the Dominions Hotel, but there was no guarantee that they would know his next address. There were difficulties monitoring his calls due to the multiple extensions at Kings College and it was decided that someone should make cursory calls to him on a daily basis, to make sure he was actually at the college.

On the weekend of 22–23 September he visited his parents at Sandhills Road, Barnt Green, Worcestershire.

On 24 September Nunn May's luggage, consisting of five crates of household effects, and six boxes and one trunk of personal effects, was due to arrive at Avonmouth Docks. Due to a dock strike these were delayed and initially arrived in Belfast. A decision was taken not to search the luggage in order not to arouse suspicions.

The intelligence gathering on Nunn May was to continue although kept at a low level. The next question was whether he would keep an important redezvous with a Soviet agent in London on the dates of 7 and 17 October as reported by Gouzenko. This could provide even more damning information, but MI5 would have to wait and see.

It became clear that any arrest of Nunn May would have to be synchronised with simultaneous arrests of all persons implicated in Canada. Failure to do so would mean that compromising documents in possession of suspects in Canada and the USA might be destroyed.

On 26 September it was reported that five packets of papers addressed to Nunn May were being forwarded by sea in the High Commissioner's bag from Canada. Prior to their despatch, Cockcroft had found in one of the packages, three copies of a diagram which Nunn May was not entitled to and should not possess. He had not submitted these documents to Cockcroft for his approval prior to departure. Cockcroft proposed that in future, no documents returning to the United Kingdom dealing with the Tube Alloys Project should be re-issued to personnel until they were re-engaged on the project. The proposal quickly became policy.

Intelligence Services met with Wallace Akers from the Tube Alloys Project again on 28 September. He was brought up to date with the Nunn May case and the continuing requirement for secrecy. A note in the files reveals that; 'he (Akers) could not be certain of Blackett', a renowned physicist. Once again Akers was reminded of the seriousness of the case and the evidence mounting against Nunn May. At a similar meeting, the possibility of planting documents received from Canada, on Nunn May, was again considered, but rejected.

With the first date of the possible rendezvous of Nunn May and a Soviet agent, looming on 7 October, the Intelligence Services, prepared the surveillance necessary for such a meeting. Special Branch were now involved in the operation. It was decided that Nunn May should be under observation from the 6 October but would not be followed to the rendezvous to avoid arousing suspicion. Two Special Branch officers, Burt and Hunter, were to monitor the rendezvous from a public house, the Museum Tavern, which was on the corner of Museum Street and had a good view of Great Russell Street, and a watch was to be kept on a telephone kiosk in Montague Street. This would enable communication between the officers and enable them to assess whether other unknown or suspicious individuals were monitoring the rendezvous.

MI5 discussed a series of possible scenarios which might take place at the rendezvous, and more problematically, what action if any, should be taken on any events which might unfold at such a meeting. They included the various possibilities, that Nunn May and a contact attended, and that documents were or were not exchanged, that one attended and not the other, and whether or not the contact could be identified, and if not, followed to an address to establish identity. There was of course the possibility that nobody would be identified as being present at the rendezvous.

The question of intervention and possible arrest was discussed. This was considered to be inadvisable since the evidence against Nunn May was not yet comprehensive. Interrogation would have to follow, and they felt they were not yet sufficiently well prepared for such a situation. It would also generate publicity which would seriously undermine the uncovering of agents in Canada, still a guarded secret.

It was decided that an arrest would only occur if Nunn May were to be seen to pass a known top secret document to an agent, but this was thought to be unlikely.

CHAPTER SEVEN

Since returning from Canada on 17 September 1945, Nunn May had been preoccupied with trying to find somewhere to live. The availability of accommodation in London after the blitz was not easy and his furniture and belongings would soon be arriving at the docks from Canada. On 26 September Nunn May's mother had written to him at King's College, with a possible contact for accommodation in London. If he were to contact a Mr Wyatt at Lloyds Bank Head Office in Lombard Street, he and his wife might be able to help.

In the meantime after a series of protracted phone calls Nunn May eventually secured accommodation at Flat 2, 4 Crane Court, Fleet Street, London EC4. This was not a straightforward arrangement, in that a journalist Ian Mackay was living there, but had gone to Paris for a short time. Nevertheless Nunn May decided to move in at the beginning of October.

On 28 September a letter watch was commenced on Nunn May's mother's house at Bedruthan, Sandhills Road, Barnt Green, near Birmingham. On 3 October a telephone surveillance on Central 1654, was initiated by intelligence at the Crane Court address.

Nunn May now began to contact colleagues in the scientific community with a view to acquiring apparatus. There appeared to be a surplus in some government departments that were no longer required after the war. He sought to acquire an electrograph via a Sir Owen Richardson, and made enquiries about the purchase of one gram of radium via Whitehall and Sir Edward Appleton of the Royal Society, explaining that he wished to follow up his work done for Tube Alloys in Canada. The cost of acquiring the radium was quoted as being in the region of £3,000. The Whitehall response whilst not being obstructive, made the point that responsibility for nuclear research was to pass from the DSIR to the Ministry of Supply. Also a committee would be established which would monitor all nuclear research work in all institutions. He also sought to purchase equipment which was not being used by the Ministry of Supply. He also made an enquiry with the AScW about the salaries of technicians and communication with people who wished to undertake a postgraduate degree and preparing the lectures for students.

On Sunday 7 October 1945 at 6:30 p.m., the first of the possible dates that had been revealed by Gouzenko, Special Branch was in place at the rendezvous near the British Museum, the place where Nunn May should meet a Soviet agent.

Special Branch reported that nothing was seen of Nunn May up to 8:30 p.m. nor was any person observed who might be keeping observation at the same place. This exercise was repeated on 17, 27 October, 7, 17, 27 November and 7 December. The result was the same on each occasion, Nunn May did not turn up and nor did it appear that anyone was there to meet him. It might have been that Nunn May no longer wished to continue his contact with the Russians.

The events of that time, between 5 September and 22 September 1945, the actions of MI5, and the people involved became clearer, in 1965.

There had been suspicions for a number of years after the defections of Burgess and Maclean in 1951 that a Soviet mole was operating at a high level in MI5. While some operations had been successful such as the exposure of Gordon Lonsdale, the Krogers and John Vassall, there remained unanswered issues which were cause for concern amongst some officers in MI5. In the 1960s, Peter Wright and Arthur Martin reviewed the history of a number of spy cases dating back to 1945, as they were now able to call upon information which had not been available at the time.

During the 1940s and up to the middle of the 1950s, the Russians used a very safe form of encipherment for all of their transmissions between Moscow and their outposts around the globe. This included separate channels to its Ambassadors, GRU, and the KGB. The volume of transmissions was vast and had been impenetrable. Furthermore Winston Churchill forebade any anti Soviet intelligence work in the UK during World War II.

After the war, the charred remains of a Russian codebook were found in Finland. An American cryptanalyst named Meredith Gardner, began to make slow progress in decoding some of the messages. The sheer volume of traffic during the war pressurised the Russians into duplicating their ciphers, which Gardner was able to exploit in decoding fragments of messages. The Americans had continued monitoring Russian messages during the war and by comparing their findings with messages sent over many years Gardner began to make progress. It was a very slow process over many years and eventually the Americans eventually shared the secret with the British. It was codenamed VENONA.

After Gouzenko's defection on 5 September 1945, an MI6 officer, Peter Dwyer was deputed to travel from Washington to attend Gouzenko's debriefing in Canada. The information gained from those interviews was relayed to London where it was received by the Head of Soviet Counter Intelligence in MI6, Harold Adrian Russell (Kim) Philby.

On 18 September, top secret files revealed the transfer of copies of the details of Gouzenko's information which had been brought from Canada by Detective Sergeant Bayfield. This information was forwarded as Top Secret by J.H. Marriott in an internal memorandum to H.A.R. Philby Esq. Philby had been appointed to set up a section designed to counter Soviet espionage operations. He was also appointed a liaison officer between the British Secret Intelligence Services and the American CIA.

We now know that Kim Philby was operating as an agent for the KGB. He would certainly have informed his Russian controller of events in Canada when another urgent problem came his way. A senior NKVD officer, Konstantin Volkov, had approached the British Consulate in Istanbul offering to reveal the names of soviet spies in

Britain in return for payment. He provided a list of the departments where the spies were active. As was normal practice, the list was sent to MI6 and its Head of Counter Intelligence, Kim Philby, who was now in a dilemma as to whether he should go to Turkey or Canada. Eventually he asked his colleague Roger Hollis of MI5 to go to Canada where he eventually interviewed Gouzenko. Philby travelled to Istanbul to make preparations for Volkov's defection. Volkov never appeared nor was he ever seen again.

After World War II, GCHQ in Cheltenham had begun monitoring Russian transmissions again. Information elucidated from VENONA in the 1960s enabled them to decode messages sent between 15–22 September 1945 through the KGB channel from Moscow to London and unravel the events of that time. On 15 September messages were being sent to Boris Krotov, in the Russian Embassy in London. Krotov specialised in running agents in Britain. The messages indicated that the GRU had encountered problems as a result of "difficulties" in Canada and they should be on their guard. However since the GRU operated independently of the KGB, it was unlikely that KGB operations would be affected. VENONA then revealed that the messages sent on 22 September 1945 from Moscow to London, adopted an urgent and elaborate tone. This was probably in response to a telegram which Philby had received from Canada on 18 September. It contained details of an unknown spy codenamed Elli, who Gouzenko had said was operating in MI5. A copy of the telegram was discovered by Peter Wright in 1965 in the MI6 files. It had been initialled by Philby two days after having received it. This would have been damaging to him personally and Philby had probably shown it to his Russian controller. It threatened Philby's continuation as a KGB agent and might possibly lead to his exposure.

Therefore regarding Nunn May, the KGB in London were in full knowledge of MI5's interest. Although MI6 operated separately from MI5, Philby always kept a broad interest in all intelligence matters and continued to receive items of MI5 correspondence on Nunn May which were pertinent. It was hardly surprising that no Russian agents appeared at the arranged rendezvous. The resources available to MI5 were limited. It has been estimated that there were at least 300 Russian agents operating in Britain at the time, compared with seven officers in MI5 delegated to surveillance duties. The Soviet network's intelligence operations threatened to overwhelm MI5. After Peter Wright joined MI5 in 1955, he was able to demonstrate that the Russian Embassy in London knew that its staff were being watched when they left the Embassy and they could identify those who were following them. In other words the MI5 watchers were being watched.

Nunn May never kept any of the proposed rendezvous dates but was making plans for his future in a post war Britain. On 12 October he received a telephone call from Mrs Wyatt to say that she had heard of the possibility of an unfurnished flat at 12 Stafford Terrace, off Phillimore Gardens, between Barkers and Earls Court Road. Surveillance of Nunn May continued on a daily basis. As an example the following is a report by intelligence services of his movements on Thursday 11 October.

> At 12.5 pm. on Thursday 11th October he left Kings College, Strand, and went to the Grill Room of the Strand Palace Hotel, for lunch. He did not make contact with any other person, and at 1.10 pm returned to the college. At 4 pm he left again, took tea at Hill's Restaurant, Strand, and then returned again to the college. He then remained at the college until 6.35 pm at which time he left and went on foot to Leicester Square. Here he had refreshments alone at the Carlton Restaurant and afterwards walked to the Strand and entered the Monseigneur News Cinema. He remained there for an hour without making any contact and then walked back to his address at Crane Court, where observation was discontinued at 8.45pm.

On 14 October Nunn May wrote to his mother in Barnt Green, from Kings College.

> Dear Mother
>   Sorry not to have written but I have been really busy what with … term starting and finding somewhere to live and running the department. I am living in a flat off Fleet Street which belongs to a

journalist who is in Paris. I understand there is a fair chance … what if he comes back but that remains to be seen.

    I got in touch with Mrs Wyatt and she has told me of … I haven't had time to look at yet but might do.

    My heavy luggage has arrived at Belfast the ship docked there. I had to send a Customs declaration out to them. I don't suppose it will arrive for another month.

    Well I must go to bed now (1.30 am) after writing my lecture next week.

    I hope you are all keeping well
    Love to all
    Alan

On 17 October 1945, surveillance had been in place at the possible rendezvous at the British Museum. Nothing of importance had been observed. This was to be expected since Nunn May was on a two day visit to Cambridge at the time, where he met up again with colleagues from the Cavendish including Engelbert Broda.

    On 23 October Nunn May telephoned a Miss May at the DSIR in Whitehall.

    He wanted to check that she had received his request for six copies of the American statement on the Atomic Bomb which would be on sale by His Majesty's Stationery Office on 26 September priced 2/6d. He asked to reduce this to four copies. He then asked if his documents had come in. The response was that there was 'a mound of them'. There was a suggestion that a Mr Aubrey would enter up all reports. Miss May said that she could not get hold of Mr Akers or Mr Cohen so they were stuck in her cupboard for days. Nunn May responded that there was no special hurry, the only point was that some of his notebooks were there. Miss May wondered if he would like to say now that he was content for these parcels to be opened, and the usual entries made for all official reports. She said his notebooks would be left more or less as they were. She asked if his notebooks were in a separate parcel. He did not know. He had left them behind to be packed up. Miss May asked if he had a lock-up. Nunn May said he was trying to get a steel cabinet with a lock. Miss May said he could really have his notebooks if he wanted, though he was not in a position to have any other Montreal reports. This confirms that Cockcroft's proposals regarding reports on the Tube Alloys Project in Montreal had been acted upon.

On 23 October, Nunn May was asked to leave the flat in Crane Court and deposit the keys at the News Chronicle offices in Bouverie Street. Ian Mackay, the previous occupant would soon be back from Paris and needed the flat. The need to find accommodation was becoming desperate and the possibility of using a camp bed in Kings College was even explored. Eventually matters were resolved for a short period by moving to a hostel for Kings College staff at the Danehurst Hotel, 16 Champion Hill, Camberwell, London S.E.5.

On 28 October Nunn May telephoned his brother Ralph to tell him that he was leaving the Ministry at the end of the week. Ralph meanwhile told him he was going into the film business in association with the Rank Organisation. Alan went on to say that he now had somewhere to live near Kensington High Street. (12 Stafford Terrace, just off Phillimore Gardens) and would be able to move there by 12 December. Alan said he would be going home for two or three days (Christmas) not more.

Alan Nunn May's mother wrote to him on 30 October:

> Bedruthan
> Barnt Green
> Nr Birmingham
> October 30, '45

My dear Alan

It was nice to get your letter. Sometimes it is far worse waiting to hear from London than from Canada. Don't ask the reason, I can't tell you. I don't seem to pick up as well as I usually do.

Couldn't ... of going to town like I did. Have you heard from everybody that we have lost poor old Jock? He was run over by a car and ... that the vet advised putting him to sleep. We miss him terribly. I quote the ... has passed to other ... as you had not mentioned it in your letter. Hope you have got used to the English rain and shall hope to hear soon that you have a paid abode and then ... home for a week.

You don't know what terrible reputation the English Government got in this ... to keep you away for 3 years and then only allow you 3 days holidays. Am sure it will make a difference to the next election.
Shall be glad to hear again soon
Best love from us both
Mother
Ted has taken us some runs in the Rolls.

'Ted' was the brother of Alan called Edward Walter Nunn May, born in 1897. He was a company director of Thomas Minto and Merry, Paint Manufacturers, West Heath, Birmingham. He also lived in Barnt Green.

On 30 and 31 October Nunn May visited Bristol to meet up with old scientific acquaintances, including Cecil Powell and Frank Smith. On 6 November Nunn May telephoned a Dr Dainty of the DSIR at Cambridge. Nunn May's feelings came to the fore as regards his treatment by the DSIR. Dainty said he had been harassed in the last fortnight and was out of favour with 'Queerstreet'.

Nunn May agreed and said 'they've given me the boot more or less. They've impounded all my notebooks, documents and everything ... after making me buy a field cabinet to put them in for safety, they now won't let me have them'.

Dainty remarked that 'he had been kicked out and told I wasn't wanted ... and further was treated like dirt by Gattacre and Perrin. I've been fuming about it ever since'.

Nunn May responded, 'I think the whole lot want treating rather roughly. I can't describe it exactly over the telephone...'

Wallace Akers was again expressing his concern about the embargo on reports from the DSIR in Canada going to Nunn May. Akers had said that it was at considerable inconvenience to himself to hold up these reports, but this would be resolved, if he was in a position to publish an order that nothing was to go to Nunn May. In order to prevent Nunn May from discovering that he was being subjected to discriminatory treatment, he (Akers) was bearing the heavy burden of having to hold up documents brought over by or sent to, other employees of DSIR. Akers was told that it was very important that he should continue as instructed.

Letter to Alan Nunn May's mother in Barnt Green, near Birmingham:

University of London
King's College
Temple Bar 5651
Strand WC9
9/11/45

Dear Mother

I am sorry to hear that you have to go … bed again. I hope you have recovered by now.

I am expecting to move to a room in Kensington which Mrs Wyatt found for me. It is impoverished but I have managed to get my … furniture delivered … have been buying basically in the second hand junk shops. Until this is ready I have been living in a hotel by the college at Camberwell – not a very aristocratic neighbourhood. I have a small room with a shilling in the slot gas fire and a hole in the ceiling – not the acme of comfort but it is somewhere to sleep.

I haven't seen Ralph since I have been back since we are both pretty busy. I haven't made any plans for Christmas but I shall like to come home for 2 or 3 days – I hope some more Canadian food will have arrived in that time but there's no hope of silk stockings I'm afraid.

Give my love to all
Much love
Alan

An extract in the intelligence files records a telegram sent by MI5 to Canada on 9 November querying how much of Gouzenko's information they would be able to use when the time came to interrogate Nunn May. They would probably need to disclose that the information had been acquired from "a well placed informant". They would not use Gouzenko's name or his code name "Corby". The point was well made that Gouzenko had never met Nunn May, but Gouzenko's information corresponded very closely with Nunn May's movements in Canada.

On 17 and 27 November 1945 surveillances was conducted outside the British Museum but again there was nothing to report.

There had been suspicions that the money held in Alan Nunn May's Bank Account in Canada was excessive in relation to his remuneration. He had closed his account before leaving Canada for the UK when it contained $4,000.

Nunn May had joined the DSIR at Cambridge on 27 April 1942 on a salary of £500 per annum. In December 1942 he went to Canada on this salary plus allowances. On 1 April 1944 his salary was increased to £680 per annum plus a bonus of £60 per annum.

On 1 April 1945 his salary was increased to £705 per annum plus the same bonus. Whilst in Canada, he received a mission allowance of $6.50 per day. All remuneration in Canada was free of UK and Canadian income tax.

Sir Wallace Akers responded to these suspicions by saying that most personnel employed by DSIR in Canada, could live on their mission allowance and save the whole of their pay. There was no evidence of Nunn May receiving excessive money in his bank account.

Letter from Alan Nunn May's mother.

> Bedruthan
> Barnt Green
> December 4, '45

My dear Alan it was a joy to receive your letter and to know you look like having a decent room or flat or whatever you like to call it. England is very behind in making any of returning sons welcome. We received a parcel from Canada from you last week and another today. Many thanks, father is certain you would … some of the soups etc … on to you and useful for cooking in your room … please let me know if … off at once. Delighted to know you will be home for Xmas, Ralph as well. Jackie is query … yet let us know arrangements as soon as poss because of what to do here. The weather has been awful – it is very kind of Mrs Wyatt to help you as ... I have her address and will write one of these days. The whole family are...

Had you heard of Ralph's ... move. Do hope it will be a success in every way. Looking forward to see you very soon my dear love from all
Mother

Letter from Alan Nunn May's father on 9 December to King's College

My dear Alan, I am sorry to tell you ... Mother has had another heart attack we have a nurse ... for nights coming in tomorrow. I had Wilkinson call today and he is very serious about her condition. We cannot offer you a bed under the circumstances and Xmas arrangements will be ... if you can come down for a day it would be well: but don't come the same day as Ralph: it would arouse suspicion in her mind. Will keep you informed of progress: but wish you had a better address: ...

Love *Father*

As a result Nunn May visited his mother in Barnt Green on 12 and 13 December. His mother died on 24 December 1945 and Alan returned home for the funeral which took place on 28 December. He then took his father down to Cornwall.

During December 1945 and January 1946, Nunn May was active in attending meetings arranged by the Association of Scientific Workers in relation to the pursuit of atomic research. The meetings were attended by leading nuclear physicists of the day who saw a need for governments of all persuasion to set out guidelines and policies for the potentially threatening developments which were taking place.

There were some physicists who were in favour of stopping all nuclear physics believing it to be too dangerous. This was the view of Dr Rothblatt from Liverpool University, who it appears had also persuaded others including Perrin and Akers to take the same approach.

This was not Nunn May's view.

Akers registered his concerns yet again to the Intelligence Services that the silence and secrecy surrounding the whole affair was difficult to sustain. Tube Alloys used external consultants for selective work and although they were forbidden to discuss their work, Nunn May had discovered their existence and thought he should be considered for such a post. This was not unreasonable and Akers found it very difficult to find reasons for refusal. Again Akers was persuaded that the situation would be resolved within a few weeks, it was a question of 'high politics'.

On and around 6 February 1946 meetings took place between Akers and Guy Liddell, Roger Hollis, Colonel Burt and Colonel Cussen of MI5. It is now known that Roger Hollis had been sent to Canada to interview Gouzenko although mysteriously no records exist of that interview. Apparently Gouzenko thought that his interviewer was in disguise and found it strange that he did not profess much interest in his disclosures. Peter Wright, an MI5 counter intelligence operator, alleged in his book Spycatcher that Gouzenko thought Hollis might be a Soviet double agent, and thought that he might have spotted Hollis in photographs from KGB files. Peter Wright alleged in his book that Hollis was a Soviet agent and despite investigations in the 1970s, the accusations were deemed to be inconclusive.

At these meetings it was confirmed that Nunn May had been a paid employee of the British Government. As such he was subject to Section 11 of the British Official Secrets Act and he was also subject to the Canadian Official Secrets Act.

Their initial proposal was that it would be desirable if he were charged under the Canadian Act. He would be questioned by British Intelligence Services and if he made admissions which would enable a charge to be brought, this statement would be submitted to the Canadian authorities in Ottawa. The Canadians would then obtain a warrant and send it to the police in the UK for execution. Nunn May would be arrested and sent to Canada under the Fugitive Offenders Act where he would be dealt with by other members of the Canadian spy network. Such an arrangement would mean that Nunn May would remain at liberty pending the arrival of a warrant, but the Intelligence

Services did not think this was dangerous.

By 15 February 1946, the Canadians had gained sufficient evidence of the disclosure of secret information from their own enquiries concerning Canadians implicated by Gouzenko, for the Prime Minister, Mr Mackenzie King, to publicly announce the appointment of Justice Taschererau and Justice Kellock of the Supreme Court, to act as Royal Commissioners. The Royal Commission would conduct interrogations and hear evidence in camera. A report would be published and prosecutions would be enacted where the evidence warranted it.

This decision by the Canadians, signalled that the time had come for the first interview between the Intelligence Services and Nunn May. It was agreed that Sir Wallace Akers would invite Nunn May to his offices at the DSIR in Shell Mex House in the Strand, London WC2 and make a room available for the interview.

CHAPTER EIGHT

On Thursday 14 February a search warrant under Section 9 of the Official Secrets Act 1911, was granted by Mr L.R. Dunne, Magistrate, at Bow Street Magistrates Court, authorising the search of rooms at King's College, London, and any other rooms which may have been occupied by Alan Nunn May.

On Friday 15 February at 2:45 p.m. in a room adjoining Room 426 in Shell Mex House, an interview took place between Lt. Col. Leonard Burt and Major Spooner of Special Branch and Alan Nunn May. On this same day the Canadian authorities made a public statement setting up the Royal Commission to investigate leakages of information to a foreign power.

Sir Wallace Akers introduced Nunn May to his interrogators but withdrew from the room when the interview began although Nunn May's later personal recollection was that it had been Michael Perrin. Before the purpose of the interview was disclosed, Nunn May turned very pale and became very distressed, he was clearly very shocked.

Eventually he recovered his composure, and began to answer questions put to him although he needed two or three minutes before answering and the responses were either 'yes' or 'no'. He commented that he felt ill at ease being alone with the two interrogators and was asked whether he wished Akers to be present, but he declined. He was perhaps uneasy in the presence of Akers, and did not want him to witness his discomfort. This may have been a bad decision, since he would have been witness to the conduct of the interview.

Burt said to Nunn May, 'We are officers of the Intelligence Corps. You are probably aware that there has been a leakage of information in Canada in connection with atomic research and that a number of persons have been detained.'

Nunn May replied, 'No. This is the first I have heard of it.'

'I have reason to believe you have been in contact with Col Zabotin, the Russian Military Attache in Canada, and that you gave secret information to an agent named Baxter otherwise known as Angelov.'

'The names mean nothing to me. I don't know what you are talking about.'

'Do you know anybody attached to the Russian Embassy or any other person acting in the interests of Russia?'

'No.'

'Have you ever given any secret information to any unauthorised person whatsoever?'

'No.'

'Are you prepared to give us any information in this matter?'

'No, not if it be counter-espionage.'

'Are you prepared to make a written statement of this interview?'

'Yes.'

Burt wrote down a statement which Nunn May read through and signed.

The interrogators did not confront Nunn May with much of the information in their possession apart from naming Angelov and Baxter, both of whom he denied having any knowledge of. He also denied any knowledge relating to the revelations of Gouzenko in Canada.

The written statement was as follows :

In January 1943 I went to work with the Department of Scientific and Industrial Research to work with an organisation known as Tube Alloys

I remained in Canada with that organisation until September 1945 when I returned to this country.

During the whole of this time I was not approached in any way by any unauthorised person for any information in connection with my work, namely atomic energy. Nor have I ever been approached by any Russian official or any person acting in the interests of the Russian Intelligence. In fact, I have no knowledge of anyone working in the Russian interest. The only person I met in Canada who could be said to be anything approximating Russian was a man named Davidson who was on the laboratory staff. There was another named ... also on the laboratory staff.

The names of Angelov and Baxter mean nothing to me – I have never heard of them. But I do know a man named Norman Veal who was on the laboratory staff. I have never been approached by any unauthorised person in connection with him.

I heard for the first time this afternoon that there has been a leakage of information in connection with atomic energy. If it means getting any of my late colleagues in Canada into trouble over this, I should feel some reluctance.

This statement has been read over by me and is true.

Signed *Alan Nunn May.*

About one hour later at 3:45 p.m., Detective Inspector Whitehead and Detective Sergeant F. Smith of Special Branch entered the room. In the presence of Burt and Spooner they informed Nunn May as to who they were and they read out the details of the warrant authorising a search of him and any premises he occupied.

If Nunn May had been shocked at the start of proceedings he must have been traumatised by a search of his person. He was being treated as a criminal.

In Room 426, they searched Nunn May and removed a Red Morocco loose leaf note book containing a diary from August 1945, including loose leaves of scientific data and two letters signed by K. Schwarzwald. And also a cheque, No. 299907 drawn on Lloyd's Bank, Cambridge, dated 10 January 1946, payable to Dr A.N. May for the sum of £190 and signed F. Grion. (The two letters were arrangements concerning a proposed lecture to be given by Nunn May on the Disintegration of the Atom at the Ilford Branch of the AScW.)

At 4:20 p.m. Inspector Whitehead accompanied Nunn May to his lodgings at 12, Stafford Terrace, Kensington, London W8. A search revealed nothing of interest.

At 5:30 p.m. Inspector Whitehead took Nunn May to King's College, the Strand and in his presence conducted a search of Room 26c. They opened a steel cabinet from which Whitehead removed a Black Morocco loose leaf note book with a diary from September 1944 and scientific notes at the end. The pocket in the cover contained:

> Document dated August 1943 marked SECRET and headed 235U SLOW NEUTRON FISSION ELEMENTS.
> Miscellaneous notes and letters
> Document marked SECRET and headed NEUTRON AND FISSION PHYSICS
> IVb Fig 1
> A 33 page typewritten document headed MONTHLY PROGRESS REPORTS NUCLEAR PHYSICS DIVISION.

The inspector left Nunn May at 6:35 p.m. to return to New Scotland Yard.

It is important to stress that no charges had been preferred nor any cautions given to Nunn May at the commencement of the interview. This had to be taken into consideration when deciding on the legality of any future prosecution.

Officers Burt and Spooner were experienced interrogators, and in their deliberations after this initial interview, were convinced of Alan Nunn May's guilt. The statement made by Nunn May revealed little of what they already knew from Gouzenko's revelations. Those revelations if true, suggested that Nunn May had lied about not knowing of any Russian contact as he certainly knew Angelov. He had been asked as a British subject if he was prepared to give all the help he could in this matter. His reply had been, 'not if it were counter espionage'.

A further interview with Nunn May would be necessary.

Nunn May was left to think over what had probably been the most traumatic day in his life. He left the premises and walked up the Strand to the Garrick Hotel where he dined alone. At 7:30 p.m. he went to the

Cameo Cinema but finding it full, took a bus to the Odeon Cinema in Kensington High Street and entered the cinema at 8:15 p.m.

For the first time, intelligence reports record that Nunn May seemed apprehensive and felt that he was being followed. He continually looked around to see if he could spot anyone.

On the following day, Saturday 16 February, he attended a conference on the "Science and Welfare of Mankind at which Professor Oliphant and Sir A. Egerton were speaking on the Implication of Recent Scientific Developments. About seventy-five people were present and they included Harry Pollitt, Professor J.D. Bernal and Josef Winternitz.

On Sunday 17 February he went to the Ballerina in Kensington High Street for lunch. Afterwards he attended a concert at the Albert Hall in the afternoon. In the evening he had dinner at the Majestic at 142 Kensington High Street and afterwards took a bus to the Odeon Cinema at Marble Arch. The film Caesar and Cleopatra had already begun so he returned to the Kensington Odeon where it was also too late to see the film. He walked to the Adam and Eve for a drink and after quarter of an hour walked home to the flat in Stafford Terrace.

These movements were reported by the Intelligence Services who commented that Nunn May was continually looking over his shoulder. He jumped on a bus at the very last moment and looked back on the platform to see if he could recognise anyone. They also thought that one of their men had been spotted.

Nunn May would have had contact with those attending the conference and did leave those premises with an unnamed man. It can only be speculated as to whether he felt able to talk to anyone about the interview, and to share his troubles. There is no record of any telephone conversations. He seems to have sought solace by escaping to the cinema and remaining alone.

After the first interview at which Nunn May had denied any wrongdoing, Intelligence Services asked Sir Wallace Akers and Perrin from DSIR to examine the notebooks which had been confiscated from Nunn May himself and at King's College.

It was Akers' view that the notebook from King's College contained material which, strictly speaking, should not be in his possession. There were reports from America on atomic research which were secret and were only seen by Nunn May in connection with his work at DSIR. There were also charts which were secret and ought not to have been retained by him.

At 11:30 a.m. on Wednesday 20 February 1946, Burt and Spooner again saw Nunn May, this time at 15 Savile Row, London W1. At his first interview he had revealed very little and it was necessary to ascertain whether he had passed on information about atomic energy research to the Russians.

Burt said, 'You have no doubt noticed by now from the newspapers that enquiries are being continued into the matter we discussed with you the other day. Additional information has since come into our possession which I would like to talk to you about.'

Nunn May replied, 'I have nothing to add to what I told you the other day.'

'We understand you had an appointment in London shortly after your return from Canada, to meet someone. It was in the vicinity of the British Museum, but I am aware however, that you did not keep it.' Nunn May did not reply.

Burt then said, 'What was the code which was to be used? You were to say to your contact, Greeting from Michael, and you were both to carry newspapers under your arms.'

'No, I did not keep the appointment, as when I returned here I decided to wash my hands of the whole business.'

'Who was the person in Canada who made the appointment for you?'

'I would rather not say.'

'Is it a fact you gave some uranium to an unauthorised person in Canada?'

'Yes, a microscopical amount.'

'Was it U233 or U235?'

'It was U233.'

'Did you give anyone any information about atomic energy research?'

'Yes, but this is covered in the Smythe Report.'

Burt then said to Nunn May, 'In order to avoid any misunderstanding and in the interests of accuracy I propose to record in writing the information you have given us. Are you prepared to make a signed statement?' He replied, "No."

Burt continued, 'We propose in any case to record this interview in writing as I shall have to submit a report about it. Perhaps you would like to vet it before we leave you, to ensure that there is no mistake.' Nunn May agreed.

He read the statement which had largely been dictated by himself to Spooner, read it several times and then signed it.

That statement is reproduced in full:

About a year ago whilst in Canada, I was contacted by an individual whose identity I decline to divulge. He called on me at my private apartment in Swail Avenue, Montreal. He apparently knew I was employed by the Montreal laboratory and he sought information regarding atomic research.

I gave and had given very careful consideration to the correctness of making sure that development of atomic energy was not confined to the USA I took the very painful decision that it was necessary to convey general information on atomic energy and make sure it was taken seriously. For this reason I decided to entertain a proposition made to me by the individual who called on me.

After this preliminary meeting I met the individual on several occasions whilst in Canada. He made specific requests for information, which were just nonsense to me – I mean by this that they were difficult to comprehend. But he did request samples of uranium from me and information generally on atomic energy.

At one meeting I gave the man microscopic amounts of U_{233} and U_{235} (one of each). The U_{235} was a slightly enriched sample and was in a small glass tube and consisted of about a milligram of oxide. The U_{233} was about a tenth of a milligram and was a very thin deposit on platinum foil and was wrapped in a piece of paper.

I also gave the man a written report on atomic research as known to me. This information was mostly of a character which has since been published or is about to be published.

The man asked me for information about the U.S. electronically controlled A.A. shells. I knew very little about these and so could give only very little information.

He also asked me for introductions to people employed in the laboratory including a man named Veale but I advised him against contacting him.

The man gave me some dollars (I forget how much) in a bottle of whiskey and I accepted these against my will.

Before I left Canada it was arranged that on my return to London I was to keep an appointment with somebody I did not know. I was given precise details as to making contact but I forget them now. I did not keep the appointment because I had deemed that this clandestine procedure was no longer appropriate in view of the official release of information and the possibility of satisfactory international control of atomic energy.

The whole affair was extremely painful to me and I only embarked on it because I felt this was a contribution I could make to the safety of mankind. I certainly did not do it for gain.

Thus Nunn May admits to having done what was revealed by Gouzenko without naming names and excluding the detail supplied by Gouzenko. It was Lieut. Pavel Angelov, Secretary of the Military Attache at the Russian Embassy who was Nunn May's contact in Canada.

As regards the U_{235}, Dr Cockcroft had already stated that U_{235} was not available in Canada, whereas U_{233} was. It was surmised that the U_{235} could have been stolen via USA sources and passed to the Russians. Uranium 235 is that isotope which is an integral part of the chain reaction which forms the atomic bomb. Nunn May was known to have visited the atomic pile at Chicago at least twice, where he could have obtained such material.

Nunn May also makes the point that what he had revealed would be published anyway, but this does not take account of the fact that he had provided technical information which the Russians would not be privy to by reading any publication. They desperately needed any materials or information on atomic energy to accelerate their programme of nuclear expansion.

At 4 p.m. on the same day that a second statement by Nunn May was made, the Intelligence Services arranged a meeting with the Director of Public Prosecutions (DPP).

They briefed the DPP with the background of the Nunn May case and drew his attention to the statement Nunn May had provided earlier that day. They also referred him to the relevant provisions of the Official Secrets Acts 1911, 1920, and undertook to provide a copy of the Canadian Official Secrets Act 1939.

One hour later the Intelligence Services and the DPP called upon the Attorney General at the House of Commons and acquainted him with the facts of the situation. It was decided that the DPP would examine the legal position from the point of view of various Official Secrets Acts as regards who had jurisdiction, Canada or the U.K. The Attorney General and the DPP concurred that the statement from Nunn May was admissible in court. MI5 were asked if they had ample material in the event of cross examination in the witness box. They said yes. The Attorney General said he would consult the Foreign Secretary and possibly the Prime Minister about the general policy decisions involved.

The following morning, Thursday 21 February, MI5 discussed further aspects of the relevant law with the DPP. He thought that Canada and the United Kingdom had jurisdiction. He requested that the following statements be obtained urgently:

a) Statement by an appropriate person showing clearly the employment of Nunn May by the United Kingdom authorities at all times.
b) Statement by an appropriate person indicating the degree of knowledge which Nunn May would have had on the matters in question.
c) Statements by Special Branch Officers Burt and Spooner.

The DPP deliberated further on the Official Secrets Acts of 1911, 1920, 1939, and on 23 February gave his opinion as to the jurisdiction of the courts in the UK to try the offences committed in Canada.

He said that under Section 2(2) of the 1939 Act, Canada had jurisdiction to deal with offences involving Canadian security. However, if a person holding office under His Majesty by virtue of appointment by the UK Government is alleged to have committed an offence under the 1911 Act, whether in this country or elsewhere and whether or not the information was secret only to a particular British possession, it is clear that the courts of this country have jurisdiction to deal with the offence. He added that if it could be established that the person concerned was the holder of an office under His Majesty and was appointed by the UK and that he acquired and communicated in Canada secret information of vital importance to the UK as well as the Canadian Government, it would appear therefore to be justifiable for prosecution to proceed either in this country or Canada.

As to the admissibility of Nunn May's statement, which was virtually a confession taken by way of question and answer, and not obtained under caution, the DPP thought this should be admitted as evidence. His reasoning was that Nunn May was interviewed by Intelligence Officers not for the purpose of investigating a suspected crime, but in the course to their duty to obtain information about an alleged leakage of information. Therefore, the Judges' Rules did not apply and the statement was admissible if it could be established that it was voluntary and not induced by promises or threats. It was taken by experienced and skilful officers and he considered that a court would be satisfied it was voluntary in this sense.

This may not be how Nunn May would eventually view it, but there had been no independent witness present to disagree.

MI5 were able to inform the Canadian authorities, that in the opinion of the Attorney General, there was a prima facie case against Nunn May based entirely on his confession. They also told them that there was concurrent jurisdiction in the UK and Canada, but the UK would prefer a charge under the UK Official Secrets Acts.

Meanwhile the Attorney General addressed a note to the Prime Minister, Clement Attlee, stating that proceedings should take place against Nunn May.

The Canadian authorities were kept up to date with the situation. A

Canadian Royal Commission was examining the soviet penetration in Canada. They had conducted numerous interviews, had taken evidence but as yet no report had been made public although various leaks to the press suggested a Russian involvement. They asked the British authorities whether they would need Gouzenko's information to support their case and whether it would suffice for this to be available via the Commission's report. It was thought inadvisable that Gouzenko should be expected to give evidence personally.

They also asked for Nunn May's statement to be made available to them, but the British authorities were only prepared for it to be read out to the Commission. They requested that no unauthorised persons should be present and that at this stage it should not be incorporated into any report. The exchange of some of these messages between the two countries involved Kim Philby.

An additional piece of information, which Gouzenko had apparently just recalled, was then sent from Canada. He said that Nunn May had been approached to nominate a scientist who could provide secret information on the project. Nunn May had nominated a Phillip Wallace, Chairman of the Association of Scientific Workers in Montreal and a known Communist sympathiser who had worked alongside him. He described Wallace as an excellent prospect for an agent, very cautious and competent.

Meanwhile, Nunn May remained free to continue his day to day activities but remained under surveillance. Intelligence Services were now convinced that Nunn May knew he was under observation and on Saturday 23 February events transpired that could have curtailed the whole operation.

Nunn May left his flat at Stafford Terrace at 12:50 p.m. He had lunch alone at the Majestic Restaurant and caught a bus to Tottenham Court Road and walked to the Patents Office in Southampton Buildings. He left the building at 3:15 p.m., walked down nearby Chancery Lane in the direction of Fleet Street, retraced his steps and caught a bus from Holborn to Marble Arch. After a few minutes he went into the underground station and whilst there made a telephone call at about 3:40 p.m. He then took a bus towards Kensington and went into Kensington High Street underground station near to where he lived and made another telephone call. He left the station, bought an evening paper, and had tea at the Majestic. At 4:35 p.m. he walked to the Kensington Odeon Cinema but it was full so he went home.

Later at 6:30 p.m. he left his home in Stafford Terrace and took a bus to Oxford Circus where he went into the underground station. After looking round he walked back up to street level, waited, purchased a ticket and then walked down to the platform. He then walked round and round and on to various platforms and was then lost by surveillance. He had managed to lose those appointed to watch him.

Where had Nunn May gone? Did he arrange to meet with someone when using the public telephone box? Who did he telephone? Why did he go to the Patents Office? Was this a deliberate diversion? Surveillance must have been alarmed. Had Nunn May disappeared— for ever? The whole operation could be in jeopardy.

On the following day, Sunday 24 February, he reappeared outside his flat at Stafford Terrace at 1:25 p.m. and his movements reverted to normal.

Over the next two days he continued working at King's College and was observed leaving the building with an unidentified man with whom he had lunch. Otherwise while not at the College he remained alone.

On Monday 25 February there was another irksome problem for the Intelligence Services to deal with. In a broadcast from Washington, a journalist, Drew Pearson, said that an English scientist who had been involved with the atomic bomb and the Canadian spy plot case, was under arrest in England. He said that he had been watched since leaving Canada and his telephone had been tapped. No names were given. A short report appeared in the *Daily Sketch*. The *Daily Mirror* quickly followed this up with an enquiry to the Home Office. Intelligence Services met with the key figures including Wallace Akers and instructed their respective Public Relations Officers to say they had no knowledge of any arrest.

On and around 28 February the British intelligence services received a message from Canada saying that they had no objection to Nunn May being charged in the UK. They expressed the wish that any arrest would be timed to coincide with charges brought against those involved in Canada as and when the Royal Commission published its findings.

A provisional date of 4 March 1946 was set on which to arrest Nunn May. The British authorities felt they could wait no longer bearing in mind the gravity of Nunn May's statement. It was thought that a remand of three weeks would be necessary and that it would be possible to hear the case in open court with the proviso that certain technical evidence might be heard *in camera*.

CHAPTER NINE

On Monday 4 March 1946, Inspector Whitehead of the Metropolitan Police was present at Bow Street Magistrates Court, where, on information supplied by Detective Superintendent Burt, a warrant was granted under the Official Secret Act 1911, Section 1 (1) (c), by Mr H. McKenna, Magistrate, for the arrest of Dr Alan Nunn May.

At 2 p.m. on the same day in the company of Detective Sergeant F. Smith, Inspector Whitehead went to Kings College and informed Nunn May of the warrant in his possession. He was escorted to a waiting police car and whilst inside the car, the warrant was read to him. He made no reply and was escorted to Bow Street Police Station, where at 4 p.m. on the same day he was charged as follows:

> On a day in 1945, he being now within the jurisdiction of the undermentioned Court in the said District, did, for a purpose prejudicial to the safety and interests of the State, communicate to some persons unknown, certain information which was calculated to be, or might be, directly or indirectly useful to an enemy, contrary to Section 1 (1) (c) of the Official Secrets Act, 1911.

Nunn May made no reply to the charge.

At 10:30 a.m. on the following day Nunn May appeared before Mr H. McKenna, Magistrate, at Bow Street Court. A brief summary of the case against him was outlined by Mr H.A.K. Morgan for the Director of Public Prosecutions. No application for bail was made and he was remanded in custody at Brixton Prison for two weeks until Tuesday 19 March 1946.

On Tuesday 19 March, Nunn May made his next appearance at Bow Street Court. MI5 was present to check for the presence of anyone who might be suspicious. It was noted that the solicitor representing Nunn May was Edgar Duchin, a well known Communist, from Johnson's Court in the Temple. He had been briefed by the AScW of which Nunn May was a member. Just in case they hadn't noticed this, MI5 were tipped off by another solicitor who confirmed this information.

The prosecution summoned Deputy Commander Burt, who on oath read out a statement as to what had taken place at the interviews of the 15 February and 20 February and in particular some of Nunn May's responses to his questioning. Defence counsel objected to the statement since Nunn May had not been cautioned and that inducements had been made to encourage him to make a statement. They suggested that Burt had led the accused into his responses. Burt went on at some length to vigorously defend the conduct of the interview. He denied emphatically that he had said that it would be to the defendant's advantage to make a statement. He had made notes of the interview at the time or immediately after. He had not made his notes with Major Spooner, Spooner had made his own notes. At no time had he warned the defendant. The objections by the Defence were disallowed and the statement signed by Nunn May was placed before the court as Exhibit 1. Defence Council requested that it should not be read out in court since there would be objection to it at a subsequent trial and publication in the press would be prejudicial to the defendant.

Next it was the turn of Sir Wallace Akers. He had prepared a statement which MI5 had approved for production in court. After preparing his draft statement, Akers in his accompanying letter to MI5, says 'I would like to ask you if it will be possible, and permitted by you, for me to make, at some stage during the proceedings, a statement about the excellent work which May did while in the organisation. Soon after their arrival in Canada the British team was condemned to a period of great frustration, through no fault of their own, and during this period May's general conduct was invaluable in maintaining the morale of the organisation. I feel that it would be only fair to mention this and I imagine that I am the only person who could say this of their own knowledge. Therefore if I could be permitted, I would like to be given the chance.'

Wallace Akers, who was on oath, read out his prepared statement in court. He explained that he was the Director of Tube Alloys in the DSIR. He explained how in May 1942 Nunn May had been employed to work in this organisation at the Cavendish Laboratory in Cambridge. He referred to the terms of employment Nunn May had signed up to, which was produced as Exhibit 2. It was made very clear that the work was secret and under the terms of the Official Secrets Act. He then said how in December 1942, Nunn May had been approached to work in Canada and again had signed up to the same conditions which were laid down. These were exhibits 3 and 4.

He described Nunn May's work in Canada and said that the information was important and since the war had been kept secret. He had read the record of the interview with Col. Burt and noted that certain materials had been mentioned. He went on to say that, 'those materials would be of use to a person to whom they were barred because they would enable a scientist to determine certain important nuclear physical data relating to those materials earlier than he would have been able to had it been necessary for him to first prepare those materials.'

He also said that, 'Most of what was known some little time ago about atomic research has now been published but only qualitatively not quantitatively. There is a strong feeling amongst scientists that the result of atomic research might not be kept as the secret of one country.'

At the end of the proceedings Nunn May's solicitor entered a plea of not guilty and reserved his defence.

On 6 March whilst in Brixton Prison, Nunn May was visited by his brother Ralph who was living at Tile House Lane, Denham in Buckinghamshire. Ralph had worked at the Ministry of Information at the beginning of the war. He was known to MI5 as a former President of the National Union of Students in 1924. On the following day he was accompanied to the prison by his other brother Edward, who lived in Barnt Green, Worcestershire.

Nunn May was also to receive a letter from his father at Ulverston and sister Mary at Barnt Green. He also sent a letter to his father. In the days that followed, Ralph and his wife visited and the question of new legal representation was discussed and arranged. His new solicitors were Kenwright and Cox, 35 Surrey Street, the Strand, London. His father returned from Ulverston to Barnt Green and expressed a wish to see his son.

On 8 March the Canadian authorities sent a telegram to MI5 indicating that trials resulting from the Royal Commission's reports would be conducted in open court with the exception of Gouzenko's evidence as his identity needed safeguarding for his own protection. They expressed concern at the need for the UK to synchronise its actions with events in Canada. They anticipated that trials of the Canadian detainees would begin after 14 March. They also raised the possibility of Nunn May being available to appear before the Royal Commission after completion of his case. Finally, they requested if a representative of the DPP could go to Canada as soon as possible, as there were a number of matters to discuss, and in the context of these events a meeting would be extremely helpful.

The response was that Nunn May had been remanded in custody until 19 March, when further evidence would be available to obtain committal for trial at the next Criminal Court Sessions due to start on 30 April. They thought there would be serious legal and practical difficulties in securing the attendance of Nunn May in Canada. Arrangements could be made for the DPP to visit Canada after Nunn May's committal on 19 March.

On 15 March the *Times* reported that the Royal Commission in Canada had named four persons involved in espionage in its second interim report. They included Fred Rose, of the Labour-Progressive Party (known to be composed largely of communists and left wingers). He was a member of the Federal Parliament and was taken into custody. The others were remanded on bail. These revelations were referred to by Ralph on one of his visits to his brother in Brixton Prison.

Up to this point no information was provided to the Royal Commission about Nunn May's activities in Canada. Ultimately a decision was made that a copy of Nunn May's statement would be made available to the Royal Commission on the understanding that it would not be published until his trial was over. The DPP, Theobald Mathew, flew to Canada, and on 29 March 1946 gave evidence to the Royal Commission on the Nunn May case.

On 26 April Ralph Nunn May visited his brother Alan in Brixton Prison. Their conversation was taken up by the defence strategy. They were both concerned that they had not yet received a copy of the indictment. Nunn May had also prepared documents in prison and was anxious that these should be collected by his solicitor. It was also agreed by both of them that the cross examination of Wallace Akers at the trial should be "a rigorous subject for his solicitor" since Akers was well informed about his work in Canada.

Nunn May also received a number of letters of sympathy and support for the position he had taken. The following is an extract from a postcard written by a Leslie Carruthers of Blanchard Hill, Jacobswells, Guildford. He was a known communist sympathiser.

> ... The only means of survival for Britain is the immediate abolition of war through the federalisation of mankind by joint possession of the destructive processes of the new molecular physics. Therefore anyone who, privy to these processes, publishes them is...
> ... a hero ... He alone is the true British patriot. This is written on a postcard in order that the Court may read it. If it is contempt of court, I invite them to imprison *me*.

Also the following telegram.

YOUR ALLEGED CRIME ADMIRABLE ACTION GOOD LUCK

This was from an Eric Joseph Gardner-Camp. He had been an election agent for the Communist Party in Chelmsford and had a criminal record.

CHAPTER TEN

With Nunn May on remand in Brixton Prison, the Intelligence Services turned their attention to identifying that person or persons who they thought might have been instrumental in recruiting Nunn May as a Russian spy.

It was clear from Gouzenko's information that this had occurred in England before Nunn May went to Canada on the Tube Alloys Project. Nunn May's statements had given no names or clue to this.

Nunn May had worked with many distinguished nuclear physicists at Cambridge and at Bristol and was familiar with many of those engaged in the work. A number of these scientists were known to embrace Marxist sympathies and had worked with Nunn May at the Cavendish Laboratory in Cambridge. This was not unusual for many of those who were working or studying at Cambridge University in the 1930s. The commencement of the war with Germany in 1939 necessitated an immediate scientific effort to support the war. The government embraced all those with outstanding ability to be a part of this effort. If this happened to include those with communist sympathies, then so be it, since the war against Germany was of paramount importance. The passage of time was to reveal that this need for immediate action resulted in the usual vetting procedures being less than satisfactory.

Therefore, there were a number of possible suspects, coupled with those whose names had been in Nunn May's notebooks, and the telephone calls and correspondence that the Intelligence Services had intercepted. They set out to trawl through the list in order to isolate those who they perceived to be the most likely suspects. The actions taken by the Intelligence Services in order to identify the person who had recruited Nunn May as a Soviet spy, centred on his movements and communications on returning to Britain in September 1945.

They admitted at the time that most of his actions were related to the furtherance of his work and they could not identify anything which was outwardly suspicious. They were left with a series of names worthy of further investigation as there was no good reason as to why Nunn May should be in contact with them.

Again during this period, Kim Philby's name appears on a number of the Intelligence Service documents to indicate that he was fully aware of the extent of the investigations.

The following is a list of some of the names Nunn May contacted when he returned to the U.K. some of whom it was thought necessary to follow up.

Professor Patrick Blackett
A leading Cambridge scientist and an expert in atomic physics who received the Nobel Prize in 1948

William Beck
The son of a well known doctor and himself trained in Medicine. He lived at 8 Regents Park Terrace, London. He gave up medicine for electronic research and was an expert in radar. During the early part of the war Nunn May had briefly worked on a secret radar project.

On 23 March 1946, Cockcroft in Canada reported that Nunn May had taken a number of reports from the Physics Library at Montreal National Research Laboratory and not returned them. The majority of these were on the subject of radar.

Lew Kowarski
Born in Leningrad on 10 February 1907. He became a French national on 16 November 1939 and entered the U.K. on 21 June 1940.

In January 1941 he was engaged as Research Physicist at the Cavendish Laboratory in Cambridge where he would have worked alongside Nunn May and Engelbert Broda as part of the DSIR. He was accompanied by his wife, Dorothea, who was born in Poland and they lived at 18 Brooklands Avenue, Cambridge.

Kowarski left for Canada on 25 July 1944, where he again worked with Nunn May and returned on 12 January 1946 and went to live at 65 Canfield Gardens, London NW6. He ceased employment with the DSIR. This address was the residence of Gessel Schkolnikoff, a Russian dentist who had come to the U.K. in 1914 and had lived at that address since 1925. He was known to be doing dental work for the Communist Party and Percy Glading, (convicted of spying for the Russians at Woolwich Arsenal in 1938), was one of his patients. It appears that Kowarski was related to Schkolnikoff. There was a strong suspicion that prior to 1940 he had worked for the Russian Secret Service. Kowarski met with Engelbert Broda and Nunn May on 14 January 1941 in London.

Kowarski returned to France but came back to England on 19 April 1946.

W.E. Van Heyningen

Was a biochemist at the Welcome Laboratories, Langley Court, Beckenham and was married with two children. He seemed to be on very good social terms with Nunn May having been invited to his house for a meal on more than one occasion. He was married with at least two children. They lived at 60 Clifton Hill, Maida Vale, London.

What was of particular significance to the Intelligence Services was that Nunn May had dinner with Van Heyningen at the Maida Vale address at his invitation on 23 February 1946. This was the same date on which Nunn May appeared to deliberately lose those following him. It was also just 3 days after he had provided his second statement.

It appeared that Van Heyningen was the only person he had been in personal contact with since his first confession on 20 February. In 1954, Van Heyningen was reconsidered by MI5 as a Soviet contact in this matter, but they could find no evidence.

Engelbert Broda

Was an Austrian physicist who arrived in the U.K. in 1938 seeking sanctuary from Nazi persecution. He was engaged at the Cavendish Laboratory to work for the DSIR and worked alongside Nunn May. The security services were suspicious of Broda. He had been an active member of the Communist Party in Vienna and remained an active communist sympathiser. They advised caution to the DSIR and a watch kept of his activities and his correspondence was intercepted.

Broda met Nunn May in Cambridge during October 1945 and again in London on 14 January 1946. Broda had also been in touch with Schkolnikoff in August 1944. MI5 asked the Chief Constable of Cambridge, D.N. Babbington, if he had any information regarding Broda's reaction to the charge against Nunn May. It is not known if a reply was received.

Broda eventually resigned from the Cavendish Laboratory and expressed a wish to return to Austria. This was viewed with alarm by the Intelligence Services at the time. No evidence was ever discovered of his implication in espionage activities at that time and he returned to Austria in 1947.

Cecil Frank Powell

A physicist and colleague of Nunn May when he worked at the University of Bristol. It was known that Nunn May had visited Powell in Bristol between 30 October and 1 November 1945. He had also worked in the Cavendish Laboratory during the twenties under Rutherford. He eventually became Professor of Physics at Bristol in 1948.

The decision was taken not to pursue enquiries about Powell and it was assumed that Nunn May had consulted with him regarding his resuming his lectureship duties at Kings College.

Phillip Russell Wallace

Was born in Toronto on 19 April 1915 and was educated at Toronto University where he was a Fellow in Applied Mathematics from 1937–40. He taught Mathematics at Cincinatti University from 1940–42 and at Massachusetts from mid 1942 to the end of that year. He obtained a post at the Montreal Laboratory of the National Research Council and worked alongside Nunn May. He was Chairman of the

Montreal Branch of the Canadian AScW.

Further information came from Canada that Gouzenko had suddenly recalled that in August 1945, Nunn May had been approached to nominate a scientist who could provide secret information on the nuclear project. Nunn May nominated Phillip Wallace. He was a known Communist sympathiser.

Wallace had not been chosen by the laboratory organisation to do selected work, but he had free access to secret information. Nunn May had been quoted as describing Wallace as an excellent prospect for an agent, very cautious and fully competent.

A telegram from Canada indicated that Wallace was leaving New York on the Queen Mary on 20 March 1946 for a few months visit to the U.K. This information had been provided by Cockcroft. Wallace was engaged to work under the auspices of Professor Mott at Bristol University. Mott knew nothing of Wallace's involvement with Nunn May's case.

It was decided that arrangements be made by Special Branch to interview Wallace on his arrival in the U.K. This was to be done with extreme caution and was more in the way of a tentative enquiry. On 8 April 1946, Deputy Commander Burt of Special Branch in the company of Detective Inspector Phillips, from Bristol, proceeded to the Physics Department at Bristol University where they interviewed Wallace. He was questioned as to whether he had ever been approached in Canada, or elsewhere, by unauthorised persons regarding the secret work on which he was engaged. He could not remember any unauthorised approach. He said he knew Nunn May very well and was astounded to hear of his arrest. The interview lasted about 15 minutes.

Burt commented afterwards that he thought that Wallace was not prepared for the interview and was extremely nervous. He also said that he felt Wallace was unwilling to discuss Nunn May in any way. Burt did not press the matter since he felt he might give away more information than he was receiving.

Prior to the interview at Bristol there had been a number of letters exchanged between the Chief Constable of Bristol, C.G. Maby and Sir David Petrie, Director General of MI5 as to whether or not Professor Mott should be interviewed to see if anything more was known about

Nunn May and his relationships with colleagues at Bristol, including Cecil Powell. There was the issue of obtaining more evidence for Nunn May's prosecution, a matter for Special Branch, and the possibility of obtaining more intelligence information, which was the business of MI5. The decision was taken not to interview Professor Mott. Later, Burt of Special Branch was to express his dissatisfaction at the way in which Bristol Police had handled his introduction to the Bristol University authorities.

Konrad Schwarzwald
Was Secretary of the Ilford Branch of the AScW and had some responsibility for arranging scientific meetings. This was to cause him a totally unexpected problem.

On 3 March 1946, while Nunn May was under close observation he was observed to throw away some papers in a waste bin. The remnants were recovered and proved to be numerous charred scraps of paper wrapped in a copy of the Evening Standard. On examination the scraps had on them what appeared to be telephone numbers on the headed notepaper of a hotel. An attempt to identify the telephone numbers was unsuccessful but one fragment suggested the name Endsleigh which could be Gardens, Place or Street. A search was made of hotels located in these possible locations. Eventually after examining several samples of note paper from different hotels, it seemed that samples obtained from the Westway Hotel, Endsleigh Street, WC1 corresponded with those obtained by MI5, as also did the typewritten characters. Special Branch visited the Westway Hotel and took away the hotel registers covering the period 1 September 1945–3 March 1946. After scrutinising the names for anyone who might be connected with the case they identified K. Schwarzwald of 101 Craven Gardens, Ilford. When Nunn May had been searched on 15 February at Shell Mex House, two letters from Schwarzwald were found on his person in a red morocco loose leaf note book.

As a result Detective Inspector Whitehead, Special Branch, with Detective Sergeant F. Smith interviewed Schwarzwald at his place of work on 24 April 1946. Schwarzwald signed the following statement.

I am a research chemist, employed, since August 1942, by Sherwood Paints Ltd, Jenkins Lane, Barking. About January 1946, I was secretary of the Ilford Branch of the ASc.W.

It was my duty to engage speakers to address our meetings, then held at the Co-operative Hall, Ilford Lane. The committee decided to seek speakers on atomic energy. On a list of speakers given to me was the name of Dr Arrol to whom I wrote. He was unable to accept, but suggested the name of Dr May who had been in Canada and was better qualified to speak than himself. I did not know Dr May, but wrote to him on two occasions. He did accept the offer, but the lecture was postponed and Dr May was arrested before it took place.

About 1 September 1945, I think it was a Saturday, I called at the Westway Hotel, Endsleigh Street, WC with Miss Jutta Scharfstein an Austrian, and registered, but in view of the attitude of the manageress we decided not to stay the night. We were only there for about ten minutes, and I cannot remember, and think it extremely unlikely, that I took any headed notepaper from the hotel. Apart from the two letters mentioned above I have not communicated with Dr May verbally, by writing, or through any other person. The first time I ever heard of him was when Dr Arrol mentioned him as a prospective speaker. Since about the beginning of February I have ceased to be the secretary of the AScW of Ilford.

Johannes Hahne

This man's story portrays some of the traumas and complications suffered by victims of war, and it serves as a reminder of the tragedy many people suffered while Nunn May was conducting his work in safety in Canada.

Johannes Hahne was a German prisoner of war in a Camp 69 at Catterick in Yorkshire. On 16 March 1946 he wrote a postcard in German to Dr A. Nunn May which was addressed to King's College, London. It was intercepted by the Intelligence Services.

The translation is as follows:

I have a question and I beg for a reply. After long investigation I could construct a new explosion motor suitable specially for aircraft and also for lorries. It works in a new way and is about 60% cheaper in production and working. Is there now in Germany a Patents Office or can I ask for a patent in a foreign country for this invention?

Hahne was born in Marchinetz, Poland on 23 July 1919, the son of a teacher. His story was that he studied engineering in Breslau and joined the Hitler Youth form 1933–34 from which he was expelled because of his anti Nazi activities.

At the end of his studies he was engaged in the Luftwaffe as an engineer and at the same time worked privately on his invention intending to sell it abroad after the war. During 1941 he was engaged in bomb disposal and was stationed at air bases in Flushing, Eindhoven, and Volkel in Holland. In 1943 he married a Dutch girl and because of his position was able to prevent some Dutch people from being arrested. He joined the Dutch underground movement but was arrested by the Gestapo in 1944 and imprisoned at The Hague-Chevingen. He escaped and was kept hidden in Overlangel, near Ravenstein until the arrival of Allied troops. He was handed over to the allies by the Dutch Underground movement because of his German associations. He had now been in a P.O.W. camp in England for a year and a half, and despite promises from a Captain Hill, that he would soon be returning to Holland or joining the bomb disposal squad, he was not allowed to return to Holland. He was also disturbed that he was sharing his accommodation with German prisoners who had been his enemies during the war. He also resented the fact that incoming letters revealed that Nazis were being released from captivity and returning home. He said that he had contracted a nervous complaint and was a completely broken man.

In order to ascertain why he had written to Nunn May the intelligence services interviewed him in the presence of a German translator at Kensington Palace on 25 April 1946.

It transpired that Hahne had tried to seek the help of his Camp Commandant in pursuing his idea of a patent. This had been unsuccessful. He wrote to the Information Bureau at Curzon House in London but the letter was returned to him. He had access to newspapers and had read the Daily Herald, Daily Mail and News Chronicle in a limited way because of his poor English. He had read about the Nunn May case in Canada. He also seemed to have read about the arrest of Canadian officials following the Royal Commission hearings. He knew Nunn May had been arrested but also thought that he had been released. As far as Hahne was concerned, Nunn May seemed to be an eminent scientist in England who could help with his release from internment, so he wrote to him.

The intelligence services accepted Hahne's explanation and that his actions were not of a sinister nature. It is not known what happened to Hahne after this episode.

CHAPTER ELEVEN

On 1 May 1946, Alan Nunn May's trial began at the Central Criminal Court, The Old Bailey in London. Sir Hartley Shawcross, the Attorney General, and Mr Anthony Hawke, appeared for the Prosecution. Gerald Gardiner, appeared as Defence Council for Alan Nunn May.

After Nunn May had pleaded not guilty at Bow Street Magistrates Court, Ralph his brother had sought a barrister who was willing to defend him. It appeared that his solicitors Kenwright and Cox had experienced difficulty in obtaining legal representation, and after the war barristers were unwilling to be involved in yet another spy case. Ralph, who was in the film business, sought the help of Sydney Box, a film producer whose office was in Guild House, St. Martin's Lane. He explained his brother's plight and was convinced of Alan's innocence. Gerald Gardiner agreed to take on the case. He was to become famous as a defence council in the trial for obscenity of the book Lady Chatterley's Lover in 1960. He was appointed Lord Chancellor in 1964. Sydney Box's wife, Muriel, was to become Gerald Gardiner's wife in 1970.

The charge before the court was,
'communicating information contrary to the Official Secrets Act, 1911, and the particulars are that on a day between 1 January and 30 September 1945, for a purpose prejudicial to the safety and interest of the State you communicated to a person unknown information which was calculated to be or might be useful to an enemy'.

Nunn May pleaded guilty to the charge.

Thus Nunn May placed himself entirely in the hands of his counsel, and that of the presiding Judge Oliver. He had already admitted wrong doing in his signed statement, but the entering of such a plea, meant there would be no opportunity for cross examination of himself or others in the witness box during the conduct of the case. By doing so some leniency might be exercised by the judge in sentencing. He would have to rely on Gardiner's advocacy skills to present his case. Gardiner may have thought that Nunn May would not perform well in the witness box. The decision would have suited the intelligence authorities very well. They could now control the presentation of information to the court. Cross examination of witnesses would be limited, including the names of those involved and they would be heard 'in camera' outside of press reporting.

Another interpretation of Nunn May's decision to plead 'guilty' was that this was an instruction by his Soviet contacts. The case would be settled quickly and therefore only the minimum would be disclosed. There would be little opportunity to pursue further information about the soviet spying activities.

The Attorney General set out the prosecution case to Mr Justice Oliver. In his preamble he described the work into atomic research being undertaken by the United States and Canada and the possible dangers to mankind. He said that it was the wish of many that this information should be shared between the nations of the world and that the United Nations could play a role in bringing this about. However it was not for anyone, including the defendant, to set himself above the laws of the country and communicate information which the Government insisted must for the time being be kept secret.

He went on to describe how Nunn May had been recruited to atomic research work, as part of a team at the Cavendish Laboratory, Cambridge in 1942. It had been explained at the time that the work was of the highest secrecy and was subject to the provisions of the Official Secrets Act and his employment was subject to those conditions.

On 29 May 1942, he had signed a document which made clear the work was confidential and that no information concerning it was to be communicated or published except by, or to, to those specifically authorised to do so.

Nunn May's move to Canada in 1943 was described where he said Nunn May had a position of considerable responsibility and was a scientist of distinction. He had access to a wide range of secret information and obtained samples of uranium used in the manufacture of the atomic bomb. It was not until Nunn May returned to England in late 1945, that information came into the hands of Military Intelligence which necessitated enquiries to be made of him. When asked about leakage of information in Canada he denied all knowledge of it. On further questioning Nunn May had replied 'not if it be counter espionage'.

The prosecution described how at a subsequent questioning, he was confronted with the fact that it was known, that on his return from Canada a rendezvous had been arranged with persons unknown, in the vicinity of the British Museum, although Nunn May had not kept the appointment. The defendant had then provided a written statement. This was read out in court, and was in fact the second statement provided by Nunn May. Whilst reading out Nunn May's statement the Attorney General did not reveal any mention of Uranium 233 or 235, nor did he mention the name of Veal.

The prosecution went on to point out that while some information revealed by Nunn May had been published, by no means all of it had. That information would enable scientists of other countries not in possession of it, to shorten their researches by a considerable time. The latter information had been given in camera by Sir Wallace Akers in another court. In March, Anthony Hawke one of the prosecuting council had a meeting with Akers to discuss what information could not be discussed in open court. He said that Uranium 235 could be referred to in open court but not Uranium 233 which was still highly secret and should not be mentioned. He also said that by giving samples of Uranium 235 it would enable others to determine data not included in the Smythe Report. Also Uranium 233 was not mentioned in the Smythe Report.

They also referred to Nunn May's statement in which he said that the affair was painful to him and he had embarked on it because he felt he could make a contribution to the safety of mankind. He had not done it for gain. They also said that about the time Nunn May left for Canada, it seemed clear that information was sent to Canada for those who eventually contacted him and obtained his information. This latter comment was part of the Attorney General's remarks, the significance of which probably failed to capture the attention of observers in court. It was of course this issue of a spy connection operating in Britain which the Intelligence Services were now desperately trying to resolve.

The prosecution summed up by saying that it had been made quite clear to Nunn May that the atomic research he was involved in whilst in the government employment was secret and confidential and he had accepted this obligation.

It was now the turn of Gerald Gardiner, defence counsel to plead Nunn May's case, albeit that he had entered a plea of guilty.

Straightaway Gardiner told the court that Nunn May wished it to be known that he had given his information to a Russian. He had not said that in his statement. Reference was made to the circumstances in which Nunn May had made his statement. He had not written it but signed it and accepted it. Gardiner said that he had interviewed those police officers (in camera in another court) involved with the statement and the circumstances in which it was obtained. His client had said that as regards it being admissible as evidence he did not wish the point to be raised and that he (Gardiner) would not pursue it.

This seems astonishing as surely Gardiner would have pursued what might be undue duress in obtaining such a statement. There was no solicitor present to vouch for the conduct of that interview. We do not know what questions Gardiner asked the police officers. The statement was damning and perhaps he felt the damage had been done, but the fact he said that, 'he would not pursue it' might suggest that it went against his judgement.

Gardiner said that Nunn May was a man of good character, a scientist of repute and a man of high principle. He said that Nunn May had not done this for money and had embarked upon this course of action because he felt it was a contribution to the safety of mankind.

He emphasised that Nunn May was working on atomic research

and not atomic bombs, a fact which had been verified by Sir Wallace Akers. Nunn May had not given away secrets of atomic bombs to another power. He suggested that the information given was not of substantial importance. It would merely have enabled other scientists to save time in their researches. He referred to Akers' comments that many scientists took the view that atomic research must not be kept as the secret of one country. He also said that his client wished it to be known that he alone was responsible and that nobody else was involved.

Gardiner then made reference to what it was in Nunn May's mind that determined his actions in February 1945, when during the war against Germany, the Russians were Britain's allies. It had been some time after that, that the Prime Minister had made statements which began to question that position.

At this point the Attorney General interjected. He said,

'there is no kind of suggestion that the Russians are enemies or potential enemies. There is no kind of suggestion that this prosecution contemplates the Russians, if indeed this information was given to the Russians as possible enemies of this country.'

He went on to say

'that once information passes out of control of His Majesty's Government ... there no longer remains control over it and it may get into the hands of enemies'.

Despite this, Gardiner referred back to what was in Nunn May's mind under the circumstances at the time. He went on to say,

'...that we had offered to the Government of Russia any technical or economic knowledge in our power which is likely to be of assistance to them. Dr May was also aware that Russian scientists with the scientists of other countries as well, had themselves made contributions to this subject and were in a position to make further contributions, and he had in mind the terms of the alliance under which the parties had mutually undertaken to afford one another military and other assistance and support of all kinds in the war against Germany, and rightly or wrongly he felt full of indignation that the promise of the communication of technical assistance which had been give to one ally, as it appeared to him, should be the monopoly of another ... He considered this discovery was one of great consequence to humanity ... In support of the fact that that was the motive which actuated him is the fact that although he had arranged to meet someone here when he returned, as soon as he learned that the Government had stated that they were themselves about to publish information he, as he says in his statement, at once decided to have nothing further to do with it.'

Gardiner's final plea was as follows,

'contrary to law, and to the orders of his government, and in breach of an undertaking which he had given some years before, at a time when he would say he could not reasonably contemplate that the government which had said that it was giving all technical knowledge and so forth to an ally would not carry out that statement, he was giving a limited amount of information before the date at which the Government subsequently decided to publish most of it of a scientific discovery of great value to humanity, in which he had participated, to a representative of a country which was at that time an ally'.

Gardiner rested his plea for mitigation on the basis that Nunn May was acting on reasonable humanitarian beliefs. It was regrettable that these could not be sustained when the government shifted its allegiances with certain allies. Any secrets revealed were of no great importance.

Nunn May was asked before sentencing whether he had anything to say.

He replied. No, my Lord.

Mr Justice Oliver's words at sentence were as follows:

'Alan Nunn May, I have listened with some slight surprise to some of the things which your learned council has said he is entitled to put before me: the picture of you as a man of honour who has only done what you believed to be right.

I do not take that view of you at all. How any man in your position could have had the crass conceit, let alone the wickedness, to abrogate to himself the decision of a matter of this sort, when you yourself had given your written undertaking not to do it and know it was one of the country's most precious secrets, when you yourself had drawn and were drawing pay for years to keep your own bargain with your country ... that you could have done this is a dreadful thing.

I think you acted not as an honourable man but as a dishonourable man. I think you acted with degradation. Whether money was the object of what you did, in fact you did get money for what you did. It is a very bad case indeed.

The sentence upon you is one of ten years penal servitude.'

The words of Justice Oliver were strident and severe. He clearly had no sympathy with what were or may have been Nunn May's humanitarian beliefs. As regards being a scientist of repute, and his high principles being recognised by others, Justice Oliver thought otherwise. Nunn May had broken promises laid down by the Official Secrets Act. He pointed out that Nunn May was being paid by the country at the time, but did not keep his part of the contract.

The horrors of the war were still uppermost in people's minds as it must have been for Justice Oliver. Perhaps he took the view that many had sacrificed their lives for the country and here was someone who betrayed it. Nunn May had refused to elaborate on his second statement and he refused to implicate others, in particular those who had recruited him in England. This was an unanswered problem for the Intelligence Services. If he had cooperated with them it might have been that the sentence would have been reduced.

The severity of the sentence set down a marker that anyone pursuing similar intentions could expect no leniency. There were numerous people who had performed undercover and clandestine operations during the war. Despite their now being engaged in peacetime occupations, they had also signed the Official Secrets Act, which as far as they were concerned remained in force. This was a reminder of the consequences of breaking that code of silence. For many, their secrets and those of the nation remained unrevealed for twenty-five years.

CHAPTER TWELVE

Alan Nunn May began his prison sentence at Wormwood Scrubs Prison, London WC2. On 20 May he wrote the following letter from there to his solicitors.

> H. Kenwright Esq
> 35 Surrey Street
> Strand
> London WC2

Dear Mr Kenwright

I am writing to ask for advice on the desirability of applying for an extension of time to give notice of appeal against my sentence. In fact it does seem to be very heavy in comparison with others for worse crimes. I have not appealed before because it seemed to me to be more of a political than a judicial decision that was needed; but I don't want it to appear that by not appealing I and my legal advisers are tacitly admitting that the sentence was a well merited one.

Of course I realise that there is a risk of an increase in sentence, though not a very bad risk in this case I imagine (they can only increase by 40%). Also I should expose myself to some more judicial remarks, I imagine that the prosecution could not bring any further evidence or insinuation. Finally my sentence would stop running while the appeal was pending.

I find it difficult to make a decision on these points from inside here. Perhaps you would let me have your advice and if you like, the

opinion of Mr Gardiner, either by letter or in a visit.
Yours sincerely
A.N. May

The severity of the sentence had clearly had an effect. It was understandable that an increase in sentence was the last thing he wanted, but he hints that politics might have had a bearing on the sentence. He refers to the judges remarks which were a searing criticism of his character and reputation, and that he would not wish to suffer further humiliation.

Imprisonment in Wormwood Scrubs, still meant that the Intelligence Services would monitor his correspondence. After a while, they ceased to copy all letters received from the family, except those despatched by his brother Ralph. All outgoing correspondence was copied and recorded.

By the 16 July after 10 weeks in Wormwood Scrubs, he was transferred to Camp Hill Prison on the Isle of Wight.

Nunn May wrote to his brother Ralph on 7 and 24 August and Ralph duly responded. He gave his brother the news of his job amongst the film tycoons of the Rank Organisation and Associated British Pictures. He had ordered, for him, a copy of *Statistical Thermodynamics*, a Russian grammar and dictionary and taken out, on his behalf, a subscription to a scientific journal. He also enclosed two packets of razor blades!!

The question of who had recruited Nunn May was still exercising the minds of MI5. An interview with Nunn May was thought to be a good idea and the arrangements and preparations for such an interview were undertaken throughout September, October and November 1946. The whole process was to be a protracted affair.

Initially the governor of Camp Hill Prison asked Nunn May whether he would agree to be interviewed. Nunn May said that he could not decide since he did not know what the interview would be about and he might require legal representation.

The interrogation officer from Special Branch, Lieut. Col. Cussen contacted Nunn May's solicitor Harold Kenwright informing him that they wished to speak to Nunn May about his connections with the Russians. Kenwright wrote to Nunn May advising him to agree to an interview in which Kenwright would be present if he agreed to talk. Nunn May's response was that he did not wish it to take place.

Marriott from MI5 was persistent and asked to see J.C. Matheson the governor of Camp Hill Prison. During Marriott's visit to the prison he left a copy of the Royal Commission report of the Canadian espionage case to be handed over to Nunn May. Nunn May eventually saw the governor, and when asked about the report, had little to say but gave the impression that he was unimpressed.

On 24 October, Nunn May was to be transferred to Wakefield Prison. Marriott of MI5 decided that he would press ahead with an interview at Wakefield Prison on 23 November. Steps were taken to ensure that Nunn May would not receive any prior warning of the interview — they intended to spring a surprise.

The interview with Nunn May took place with Marriott and Lieut. Col. Cussen in attendance. They initially took the approach that if May or persons acting on his behalf were seeking a remission of his sentence, the full facts of the case would have to be established. They were there at Wakefield to give him the opportunity to give a full account of the case.

Nunn May listened without comment.

Nunn May said that by making any statement he would forfeit the support of his friends and advisers. Also he would not make any statement without his legal adviser being present.

They did not press him further and said that if he changed his mind they would see him again, otherwise no further approach would be made. The interview lasted about forty-five minutes. Afterwards they chatted informally.

MI5 formed the opinion that Nunn May mistrusted them and the police. They also thought that those implicated were personal friends of Nunn May. Any remission would lend suspicion that he had betrayed them. He was reassured that he would not be required to give evidence in a court of law.

They asked him if he had any views on the Royal Commission Report in Canada. His only comments were that there was a lack of scholarship in its content and that it seemed to him that they could not make up their minds whether he had done it for financial or ideological reasons.

More tellingly, the request that he should reveal the details of how he had been drawn into the case, indicated to him that the prosecution had an incomplete case. Cussen and Marriott corrected him on this, and decided it would be advisable to bring the proceedings to a close. They were anxious; Nunn May clearly resented the Intelligence Services and might utilise any weakness in the prosecution case to place the authorities in an embarrassing situation.

They concluded by saying that there would be no objection to reporting the interview to his solicitor and brother Ralph, except for certain details raised by Cussen at the beginning.

Afterwards Cussen and Marriott felt that the interview had taken place in a friendly atmosphere. They also expressed the opinion that Nunn May was not the disinterested international minded scientist which his colleagues represented him as being. They thought he was wicked and criminal.

Despite the refusal of Nunn May to cooperate, they remained hopeful that in future, if a solicitor were present, he would be willing to talk. They communicated with Kenwright, and stressed that consideration of a remission for his client would necessitate full disclosure of all the facts, although there could be no guarantees.

Nunn May lost no time in writing to his brother on the following day.

24 November 1946

Dear Ralph,
    Many thanks for your letter. There will be a double visiting order enclosed with this for you and Jackie. Mary and Father came (I think) last week. It was good to see them. They can tell you that Saturday is rather a crowded day, but better that than none of course.

For once I have some news. Yesterday (Saturday), I was called into the Governor's office and left with two (anonymous) gentleman, one of whom turned out to be same who had called on Kenwright and who seems to be an old friend of his. He held forth at some length, to much the same effect as he did to X, ending by saying that he could not say that refusing to say anything would not count against me. Nevertheless anyone asked to report on the case must feel that as it stands it is incomplete; certain aspects weren't clear; there was a gap etc. After listening to all this I pointed out that I had been asked through the Governor of Camp Hill whether I would talk to them. I had said "not without legal representatives present" and after receiving a letter from K, and considering its implications I had decided not to see them – to drive home the point. I also pointed out that whereas K had written that "I should not be called on to give evidence" they had not at *this* talk said anything about anything involving evidence at all. He replied that he quite saw my point, but felt so strongly that the public interest etc. that he had been authorised to approach me in this way. They then asked had I seen the Canadian blue paper? Yes: the Deputy Gov. at Camp Hill had lent me a copy — apparently at their suggestion. I pointed out a few trivial errors in it like the mis-spelling of my name and refused to agree that it was, on the whole, a sound piece of work.

The whole thing was then gone over with some variations – da capo. At the end the other man asked what I felt about the other Canadian cases, were they justified? I refused to discuss this, and K's friend agreed it was an improper question. After repeated assurances and a statement that I might communicate the whole thing to you and Kenwright they went; empty handed, and with a trace of flea in ear. They said that they would not come again unless I asked to see them, I assured them that that was most unlikely. I don't know how the idea has got about that I am a natural born squealer or copper's nark, or even that I have anything particular worth listening to, to squeal about. Their main argument; of saving innocent youth from "corruption" of the same sort; is quite inappropriate. In short, I don't want to have anything to do with these gentry, they are bad company.

I'm afraid this dispatch hasn't left any room for small talk which will have to be abbreviated. No clarinet reeds please, because no clarinet, but music yes! Letters once a fortnight. The rest wait till I see you.

Yours ever

Alan

This letter would suggest that Nunn May was pleased with himself at dismissing his inquisitors. He had no respect for them or their motives. He shows no regrets as regards his actions and his political beliefs remain unchanged. There are no regrets as to how this might have affected his country. There is a hint of intellectual superiority with a total disregard for those who fail to match his ability.

The idea of springing a surprise on him was presumably to catch him off guard but it failed. Nunn May was a clever man and he was not to be undone by such tactics. It appears that Nunn May was not introduced to his inquisitors unless their names were deleted when the correspondence was vetted. He found them shady characters and not to be trusted.

Marriott and Cussen's acerbic comments afterwards could have been a reflection of their annoyance at a lack of success. They had spent a great deal of time preparing for the interview without any substantial progress.

Amongst those who were to receive a report of the interview, was Kim Philby, liaison officer between the British Secret Intelligence Service and the American CIA. Philby replied expressing his regrets. Perhaps Philby had a wry smile when he ended his note by saying, 'We will naturally be very interested in anything you may obtain'.

During the months after Nunn May's trial, the AScW discussed ways in which they could approach the Home Secretary with a view to reducing the length of his sentence. They prepared a long draft which listed Nunn May's scientific achievements and the respect in which he was held in the scientific community. They argued the case for disclosure of scientific information to all nations, and that Russia had been an ally of this country during the war.

They also said that to say he had done this for money was preposterous. They went on to comment that imported whiskey into Canada was frequently wrapped in layers of paper and that the money could be concealed in this way without his knowledge. They also said that the sum involved of 200 dollars was negligible in relation to his salary.

As regards signing the Official Secrets Act, he had not sworn on oath that he would preserve secrecy in his work. He had simply signed a statement to the effect that he knew the penalty for not doing so. May served his country by trying to redress the balance of military power in the world today. May had done great service to his country ... and as a leader of research in nuclear physics ... Why should it be supposed that May was inconsistent according to his own ideals in giving information to the Russians? They noted that in the Atomic Energy Bill being placed before Parliament at the time, the maximum penalty for a similar offence would be five years imprisonment.

The draft was to be placed before a committee at the AScW for future action.

In the House of Commons on 17 May, W.J. Brown, Independent M.P. for Rugby, asked Mr Chuter Ede the Home Secretary to review the sentence passed on Nunn May. He replied that he saw no grounds to interfere with the sentence. Brown would not be deflected, and said that Nunn May was not a common criminal nor a traitor in the ordinary sense of the word. His sentence was heavier than that passed on others who had committed more serious offences and would he therefore review the sentence. The Home Secretary would not change his mind. He said Nunn May could appeal against the sentence, but he remained unsympathetic, as were the rest of the House.

An item of correspondence dated 21 May 1946, which was sent after Nunn May's imprisonment told of an alleged meeting in which had involved him with a Dr Karl T. Compton, Chairman of the United States Radar Mission and Rear Admiral Julius Furer, co-ordinator of Research and Development for the United States Navy. This was said to have occurred at Great Malvern, England, site of an important radar laboratory.

Compton saw Nunn May's name in the publicity surrounding the case and thought this was the person who had accosted him asking questions about the Mark 24 mine. This was a top secret United States Naval development which should not have been known to such an individual and more strangely had nothing to do with the radar work at Malvern. He thought the newspaper descriptions of the time matched those of Nunn May and when shown a photograph of him was certain that this was the person who had approached him. The date on which this meeting took place was either 7 or 8 May 1943.

This information was forwarded by John. A. Cimperman, FBI liaison officer at the American Embassy in London to Roger Hollis, Head of MI5. The ramifications of the Nunn May case had alarmed the FBI and they harboured serious concerns regarding the reliability of British security services and in particular, what they saw as an ineffective vetting procedure for all those involved in secret work.

MI5 were able to reply with conviction that Nunn May had gone to Canada in January 1943 and remained there until September 1945. The supposed identification of Nunn May was incorrect.

The FBI accepted this, but not without remarking in a further letter to MI5, that it would have been possible for him to have made a flying visit to the United Kingdom during that time. They acknowledged that since Nunn May's Canadian bank account showed withdrawals in person on the dates in question, this was very unlikely. This response to MI5 appeared to suggest that they, the FBI, were meticulous in the way they followed through on enquiries.

On a lighter note Nunn May received a letter in September 1946, from an occupant of the flats at 12 Stafford Terrace, Kensington, London, where Nunn May resided at the time of his arrest. The writer was a journalist on the periodical *John Bull*, and in the letter relates to gossip surrounding the occupants and in particular Elsie Johnson, the landlady. He tells of the good old times at Christmas parties, good food, and of what was a 'Bacchanalian revel' of a birthday party. The lady sent her love. As a commentary on the time the writer reveals that thousands of squatters were moving into unoccupied blocks of luxury flats.

On 31 December 1946, Nunn May wrote to Cecil Powell, Physics Lecturer at Bristol University and formerly a working colleague. He thanked Powell for his Christmas cards and said he had received 170. Some of these were from AScW branches and other trade union branches. The prison food at Christmas seemed reasonable and the inmates had staged a pantomime. He had compiled a crossword with a prize of twenty cigarettes which had proved too difficult to solve and did not increase his popularity.

He discussed a scientific paper he had collaborated on with Powell and asked him to go ahead with submission rather then sending him a copy for revision. He was receiving copies of Nature, Physics Review and Science Abstract, was learning Russian and reading classical literature. He was happy to be involved in looking after evening classes and issuing periodicals and was thinking of starting a class in elementary science.

There was also a suggestion that he might be able to pursue some form of physics experimentation in prison but this would need to be sanctioned by H.M. Prison Commissioners.

He had now completed one tenth of his sentence and seemed to be growing accustomed to prison life which he referred to as radioactive decay. He was reassured by having his own cell, and was not enamoured of contact with other prisoners.

In another letter to a Professor Paneth on 14 January 1947 he refers to his job in the educational office and of doing some typing. This contrasts with his having been a tailor at Wormwood Scrubs and a stencil cutter at Camp Hill on the Isle of Wight plus inevitably sewing mail bags and scrubbing floors. He was able to read about developments in physics and the discovery of new elements. He had been given permission to write a book which was to include information on radiation physics and its use for chemists and biologists.

The sentence of penal servitude means prison with hard labour but the letters would suggest that he was able to avoid physical hardship.

On 10 February 1947, he wrote to his father congratulating him on his forthcoming marriage which would take place sometime between Easter and Whitsuntide. He told him that he hadn't heard from his brother Ralph since Christmas but had received a large parcel of music, however his supply of razor blades was now running low.

On 25 February 1947, he wrote to Ralph. He comments on the weather (one of the worst winters on record), and is obviously agitated that correspondence and scientific journals had ceased to arrive and he is dependent on books and periodicals from Leeds University. He puts in a desperate plea to be sent various scientific books and tables if he is not to stagnate. He asked his brother to include him when purchasing a wedding present for his father and to take the money out of his bank account.

His sister Mary who had been living with her father at Bedruthan, Sandhills Road, Barnt Green, had written to him saying that she was 'glad to be away from Bedruthan' and living in Calthorpe Road, Edgbaston, Birmingham.

Before Easter of 1947, Nunn May was moved to Leyhill Prison in Gloucestershire. His letters tell of this being a much more amenable place to be incarcerated than Wakefield. Visits were much more flexible, (food could be brought in by visitors) and there were trees and grass to look upon, opportunities for dialogue with others and a piano for him to play. He took the opportunity to commence gardening at a small plot outside his window. He also expressed his satisfaction at being visited by Dr N. Kemmer, Lecturer at Cambridge University whilst at Wakefield. Again, he asked Ralph to try and get him a Russian Dictionary, more sheet music including Beethoven Sonatas and Bach piano arrangements.

The movement from one prison to another seemed to cause chaos in the system as regards the receipt of journals and correspondence and he openly admits to becoming irritated and cantankerous at his inability to get on with his research. It was always Ralph who was called upon to try and sort out the problems and he was often given clear instructions as to how to contact various bookshops in order to put things right.

The following letter illustrates that being in prison doesn't entirely separate one from the progress of the family.

                              To No 132 May A.N.
                              H.M. Prison
                              Leyhill
                              Falfield
                              Gloucestershire
Bedruthan
Barnt Green
Nr Birmingham
1st April 1947

Dear Alan
        It seems a long time since I heard anything from you or about you.: I should be glad to hear, whether you find life any better in your new milieu. It seems it should be possible to visit you from here and get back the same day provided one had the use of a car. I have heard nothing from Ralph either: but gather from Ted that he has got another house and will be moving in about a week's time and Mary is spending most of her weekends on visits to her friends, is going the next (Easter) to Bibbie's. She thinks I am doomed to perdition and takes every opportunity of pointing it out! However we are going to get married on the 19th down at Ripple, near Upton on Severn, and going to live in Cornwall at May's for 10 days: and after that hope to settle down here: and Mary will be welcome to live with us, if she recognises the facts. We have been lucky in having no damage from snow or floods: apart from one burst pipe: parts of the country must be in a ruinous mess.
    Well, write to me when you can
    With love
    Father.

It appears that Mary was unhappy at the prospect of living with her father's new wife. Shortly after this letter she seems to have contracted shingles and had to go into hospital. She had to cancel a visit to Alan at the prison. Visiting orders had to be applied for by the prisoner in advance and it was not easy to change the arrangements. Alan wrote to her in an attempt to raise her spirits describing his garden at the prison and the progress of his lettuces, onions and radishes. He was pleased that the wedding reception had been a great success.

Nunn May's scientific output was beginning to put a strain on those whose job it was to transcribe his handwriting for the benefit of MI5 – usually the job of the governor or deputy governor. Nunn May admitted that his handwriting was often illegible and the scientific information was unintelligible and barely readable by them. It probably amused him to think of their struggles to copy his scripts, and might well have done it for them if asked.

The words asymmetry in fission, in relation to integral calculus and the word meson probably seemed dangerous to non physicists – mesons were newly discovered particles in atomic physics.

The question of the length of Nunn May's sentence had not been forgotten by many scientists. In June 1947, a letter was written to the Home Secretary, Chuter Ede, to ask if he would receive a deputation to discuss the issue.

The deputation was to consist of Professor Blackett FRS (Professor of Physics at Manchester University), Professor Chapman (Professor of Mathematics at Cambridge), Dr C.D. Joad (Head of Philosophy at Birkbeck College, London), Dr N. Kemmer (Atomic Scientist in the Cavendish Laboratory and a colleague of Nunn May in Canada), Mr W. Lawther (President of the National Union of Mineworkers), Professor Pelerin (Professor of Applied Mathematics at Birmingham), Mr J.B. Priestley (Novelist), Mr Jack Tanner (President of the Amalgamated Engineering Union), Mr H. Thompson (Solicitor), and Sir Robert Watson Watt FRS (developer of radar).

Consultations between MI5 and legal opinion at the Home Office as to the justification for Nunn May's sentence were commenced again. The length of sentence was discussed in comparison with that of Douglas Springhall, a founder member of the Communist Party in Great Britain, who had been convicted of passing classified information on anti radar devices to the Russians and whose sentence was seven years. It remained the view that Nunn May had passed on information of a more serious nature namely atomic science.

The argument that most of Nunn May's revelations had been published did not alter the fact that they would have given a foreign power a significant advantage by reducing the time taken to reach a similar stage. It was also reiterated that Nunn May had refused to reveal to whom he had passed his information and by doing so, 'he is quite unrepentant'. If Nunn May had a duty to be bound by the Official Secrets Act, why did he not resign his post and make public his concerns. What did Nunn May think the Soviets were going to do with the secrets he passed on and would this not ultimately affect the U.K?

The deputation presented its submission for a remission of sentence on 2 August 1947. The Home Secretary refused any plea to reduce Nunn May's sentence.

From July to December 1947, Nunn May settled to life in the open prison at Leyhill. He was receiving his periodicals and scientific journals and was working hard on collecting material for a scientific publication, to which the Home Office had no objections. He wrote letters to his sister Mary and his father. Along with his duties in the library, he was assisting with preparations for the Christmas concert. He also took care of the cat whose kittens made a home in one of the library cupboards. He commented that time was passing quickly.

The prison deputy governor reported to MI5 that his demeanour remained reserved, with no sign of any change in attitude, but was always pleasant.

He was featured in an article which appeared in the Evening Standard during December 1947. Rebecca West wrote a series of articles about traitors and published a book in 1949 called, The Meaning of Treason, in which she was scathingly critical of Nunn May's motives. The headline of the newspaper article was 'His betrayal may harm us yet...' and she referred to him as a fatuous and gifted scientist who sold atom secrets and betrayed himself. She compared his actions, ideals and appearance with William Joyce who had been hanged in January 1946.

He wrote to his brother Ralph in January 1948 regarding the possibility of bringing libel proceedings against Rebecca West which after some thought he discounted. He said that he would only contemplate doing so when released from prison and with freedom to choose his legal representation. He said that his legal representation in prison was unsatisfactory, that he would certainly not use Kenwright again, and that he had heard nothing from Kenwright in relation to the newspaper article. Nunn May was clearly resentful of his solicitor at his trial and did not think he had performed his duties properly.

On 30 January 1948 Marriott from MI5 wrote to the deputy governor at Leyhill saying that in future he would only require copies of Nunn May's incoming or outgoing correspondence if they were thought to be of particular significance. He would like to be informed of the names of visitors who were not members of Nunn May's family. Of course he would wish to know of any change in his general attitude to his case.

ABOVE:
Alan Nunn May. The photograh on the right taken after his release from prison.
(Topfoto)

ABOVE:
The May family c. 1917. (Courtesy of Diana MacDonell)
Standing, left to right, Edward (1897-1964), Ralph (1902-80).
Seated, left to right, Alan (1911-2003), Mary Annie (1870-1945), Mary (1908-2000), Walter (1871-1950).

ABOVE:
Research Staff at Montreal Laboratory in 1943. Nunn May is standing on the far right. Standing left to right: *A.M. Munn, B.L. Goldschmidt, J.W. Ozeroff, B.W. Sargent, G.A. Graham, J. Gueron, H.F. Freundlich, H.H. Halban, R.E. Newell, F.R. Jackson, J.D. Cockcroft, P. Auger, S.G. Bauer, N.Q. Laurence, A. Nunn May.* Seated left to right: *W.J. Knowles, P. Demers, J.R. Leicester, H. Seligman, E.D. Courant, E.P. Hincks, F.W. Fenning, G.C. Laurence, B. Pontecorvo, G.M. Volkoff, A. Weinberg, G. Placzek.*

BELOW
Left: *Gerald Gardiner QC* (Topfoto)
Centre: *William Skardon* (Spartacus Educational)
Right: *Igor Gouzenko, cypher clerk* (Google Images)

Birmingham Gazette

No. 31,768 (205th Year) — LIGHTING-UP TIME 6.22 p.m. — TUESDAY, 5 MARCH, 1946 — ONE PENNY — CITY EDITION

SECRETS CHARGE AGAINST A MIDLAND SCIENTIST

Taken from College by Scotland Yard Men: In Court To-day

DR. ALAN NUNN MAY, B.A. (Cantab.), Ph.D. (Cambridge), a lecturer on physics at King's College, Strand, London, was arrested yesterday and will appear at Bow-street Court, London, this morning charged under the Official Secrets Act. He was taken into custody by Scotland Yard Special Branch men when he had finished a lecture at the college.

Dr. May was for a while engaged on research in atomic development in Canada. Some time ago he returned by air from Canada. His home, when he is not living in London, is with his brother, Mr. W. F. May, of Sandhills-road, Barnt Green, near Birmingham. He is 34, and is described as a university reader, of Stafford-terrace, South Kensington.

His father's home is also May was not on the visit, which reads: "If a person at Barnt Green. Dr. May to the U.S. when he him for any purpose prejudicial which is calculated to be was brought up in the the lives a member of the to the safety, or or if intended village, and went to a a British atomic b o m b interests of the State to be directly or indirectly famous B i r m i n g h a m mission. obtains, collects, records, useful to an enemy, he school, then to Cambridge. Dr. May is charged publishes, or communi- shall be found guilty, and University. He is known to Prof. under Section 1, Sub- cates to any other person felony, and shall be liable Oliphant and Dr. P. Moon section (c), Paragraph (c) any secret official code, on conviction on indict- both of Birmingham. the Official Secrets Act, word, or password or any term not less than three University Prof. Oliphant 1911, as amended by the sketch, plan, model, years and not exceeding and last night that Dr. Official Secrets Act, 1920 article, or note or other seven years.

Franco Promised to Enter War in 1940, Says U.S.

PLANNED WITH HITLER A BLOW AT GIBRALTAR

IN June, 1940, Gen. Franco promised Hitler and Mussolini he would enter the war against the Allies, and captured German documents issued by the State Department of which is given at New York...

Break Not Yet Likely

Spain's Reaction will be Watched

A British break with Spain is not ruled out...

NO DECISION ON LENGTH OF COMPULSORY SERVICE—Premier

Government's Aim: Forces Down —BUT NO "RISKS"

DIRTY MEAT ALLEGATIONS

Butcher President in Birmingham

...to 1,200,000 by December

MR. ATTLEE, opening the two-day debate in the Commons last night, announced that the Government's plan is to reduce by the end of this year the strength of the Armed Forces to 1,100,000 men and women, with 184,000 men in training.

The numbers were planned to be: Navy 170,000, Army 650,000, and R.A.F. 275,000.

Conscription For-Two Years?

CHAPTER THIRTEEN

As far as Nunn May was concerned, he was occupying his time with his studies, receiving visitors, and was altogether content with conditions at Leyhill as they were more congenial than those at other prisons. It was after all a reasonable place to serve out one's sentence.

That is until the 25 March 1948, when an anonymous note was found in the post box used by the prisoners at Leyhill for depositing mail for censorship.

The note said:

> As a Britisher I know it is my duty to let you know that there is a scheme afoot to organise the escape of Nunn May from the prison and to safely transport him from the country to the other side of the Iron Curtain the Russian occupied part of Germany.
>
> Mr Springhall has the arrangements in hand, which may take some time, but it may not, for our safety as a country this matter should not be taken too lightly, and should be investigated at once.

This referred to Douglas Springhall, a founder member of the British Communist Party who was serving out his seven year sentence at Leyhill for passing classified information concerning the anti radar device WINDOW via an Air Ministry clerk called Olive Sheehan. Springhall had been instrumental in fostering the development of communist sympathisers at the Cambridge University in the early thirties. Nunn May had of course met Springhall prior to his leaving for

Canada. It would have been only natural for him to seek conversation and solace from someone who was sympathetic to his political views.

It would have been fairly straightforward to confront Springhall with the allegation, but unfortunately he had been released from Leyhill on 19 March 1948 – six days before. Thus with Springhall unavailable, they pursued those inmates in the prison who might be responsible. An investigation was launched into the handwriting of the note, which was compared with samples of the writing of all prisoners at Leyhill.

MI5 were kept informed of progress and had learned from Sir John Cockcroft, Nunn May's former boss, that no possible harm would be done if Nunn May were to escape to Russia. This was no doubt reassuring to MI5 and the Home Office, but any escape would still be acutely embarrassing. Therefore, before the investigation could be completed, on 5 May 1948 less than two weeks after discovery of the note, Nunn May was transferred back to Wakefield Prison.

The investigation of the affair was conducted by Detective Inspector Whitehead of Special Branch who had searched Nunn May, his place of work and residence and subsequently arrested him at King's College. The investigation revealed that a prisoner at Leyhill called G.H. Parry, had overheard a conversation between Nunn May and Springhall. It was alleged that the following conversation took place:

> **Springhall**: I shall not move up North for a while yet because they may follow me.
> **Nunn May** agreed
> **Springhall:** I can quite safely say that you will not be here in six months time.
> **Nunn May:** Yes
> **Springhall:** Then we shall see how good the iron curtain can be.

It appeared that Parry repeated this conversation to another prisoner H.J. Thomas who said, 'I won't let the bastards make atomic bombs to blow up my family. I shall tell the governor'.

Despite the confines of prison, many prisoners were unsympathetic to fellow inmates who they viewed as traitors and felt that they needed to be exposed. Thomas wrote the anonymous letter (confirmed by Forensic Scientists at Cardiff), helped by Parry, who said that he had not favoured this course of action, although Thomas denied writing the letter on questioning. It was Whitehead's view that Parry's version of events was substantially true and Thomas was a liar although the actual words reportedly overheard between Springhall and Nunn May were not considered reliable.

As far as the Home Office was concerned the matter was closed and Nunn May was safely locked away in Wakefield Prison.

In July 1950, Parry, who by then had been released from Leyhill, wrote an angry letter to MI5 concerning the affair. He said that in his view, Springhall and Nunn May were the Governor's favourites. After the affair, he said that, despite all the assistance given to MI5 he and Thomas had been treated shabbily by the Governor of Leyhill. He resented the fact that his actions had not earned him any remission on his sentence and even worse, it seemed to have been held against him. He was angry that those of a communist persuasion seemed to receive special treatment at Leyhill. It appeared to him that the good jobs in prison and any with special privileges always went to the communists.

Nunn May wasn't interviewed nor given any explanation for his transfer back to Wakefield Prison. He must have been distressed and his state of mind in turmoil. What he thought would be a reasonable existence for the rest of his sentence, would revert to the grimness of a secure prison. He had so far kept his countenance and resolution, perhaps this would break his resolve.

Ralph Nunn May wrote to the AScW pleading on his brother's behalf for any possible help. He noted that the Prison Service could move prisoners from place to place without explanation. Surely it was unusual that his brother was being moved to Wakefield from an open prison unless, that is, he had attempted to escape or misbehaved himself in some other way. Ralph knew nothing of the alleged conversations with Springhall.

Probably Springhall thought he was helping Nunn May and the common cause of communism, but his intervention was disastrous and perhaps it was just as well that Nunn May knew nothing of the reasons for his transfer.

In July 1948, two months after his transfer, Ralph wrote to his brother Alan expressing his commiserations. His enquiries via officialdom regarding the reasons for Alan's transfer had not produced any answers. His only explanation was that this was an act of retribution for the Soviet blockade of Berlin, which was taking place at the time and was being relieved by a massive airlift.

In February 1949, Marriott from MI5, wrote to Major Guise-More, the Governor of Wakefield Prison. He asked about Nunn May's current attitude and demeanour and whether he thought a further attempt at another interview might release the information about who had recruited him as a Communist agent while in Cambridge. It had been eighteen months since the last unsuccessful attempt had taken place.

The view of Guise-More was that Nunn May remained introspective, withdrawn but polite. Guise-More did not hold out much hope for any change in Nunn May's attitude to another interview. Marriott persisted however, and he made arrangements for a further interview. The person chosen to conduct the interview was William James Skardon. He was a pipe smoking former policeman who had experience of war time interrogation. He was now the chief interrogator for MI5, popular with his colleagues, and to quote Peter Wright 'with the air of a trade union shop steward about him'.

On 21 March 1949, William Skardon interviewed Nunn May at Wakefield Prison. The following is extracted from Skardon's report:

> The Governor was a little concerned as to whether he should carry out the normal routine laid down by the regulations and ask May whether he was prepared to accept a visitor, and if so to caution him that he need not answer any questions. Upon reflection he decided to leave this task to me, and May was brought to the Deputy Governor' office, which was placed at my disposal for the interview.
>
> I told May at once that I represented the Security Service and that the Governor had requested me to make the two points mentioned above. May replied that he was quite prepared to stay and listen to

me, and we thereupon embarked upon a conversation which was by no means one sided. This lasted for about 90 minutes and was of the friendliest character, but the only real information that I could obtain was that his recruitment, if that be the right word, took place literally a few hours before he left England for Canada and that the individual for whom I might be looking in this connection was well out of my reach. I think it would be unfair to infer too much from what he said, but I gained the fairly distinct impression that the individual to whom he referred was a member of the Soviet Embassy, and I also gained the feeling that this individual followed him to Canada. There are however no firm grounds for this expression of view.

I put forward various arguments which I thought might persuade May to be forthcoming as to the earlier details of his Soviet associations. In response I received only the meagre details outlined above. His point was that he could not bear to be a squealer. He despises such people and would rather serve his normal prison sentence that gain any advantage by – as he put it – talking out of turn. He is obviously a man of some character; equally he is a difficult and lonely sort of individual, and he was not much impressed by my argument that by indicating the individuals responsible for his defection he might save others. He said that all the facts have been fully reported in the official publication of the Canadian spy case, anyone was free to learn the lesson himself.

We go on to the question of motive. May told me that he considers himself to be a Socialist, that he is pro British, has never wished to harm his country and has never been anxious to assist any other country. On his release from prison he hopes to settle down into a useful life in this country and not be harassed by MI5. He claims that he did no damage to his country or its interests by the actions which led to his imprisonment. He explained at some length how he was sent down to Chicago by his superiors in Canada to work in the American development plant, and he was told unofficially to keep his eyes and ears open and to report back anything interesting that he might discover whilst in the USA. On his return his superiors told him that he must not prepare a written report on these discoveries as it would be extremely embarrassing to the British Government in their relationship with the American State Department.

May says that the information which he passed, on a dirty piece of paper, at a street corner and the samples of uranium which he handed over, were insignificant details connected with his work, and that his only object was to gladden the hearts of the Soviet authorities by telling them that the atomic bomb was a really worth while weapon and a practical possibility, and not merely the figment of some journalistic imagination. He stressed it would be quite impossible to impart any useful information on the subject of atomic research even to an expert physicist, in less that six months in a laboratory. The whole subject was so complicated and experimental in character that a mere message or a chance meeting could provide no information that could possibly be of the slightest assistance. He recognises that to break faith at all was wrong, but is puzzled to know why other people who seem to have been more actively engaged in really subversive activities received much shorter sentences. He quite saw my point that he was a man of specialised training and in an extremely trusted position, and that therefore his offence was more serious. Perhaps the only argument that affected him in any way at all was my suggestion that if he did not indicate the persons responsible for his downfall, I should be left to browse amongst the names of his friends, associates and colleagues, perhaps to the unfair disadvantage of one of them. He said that he had always been sensible of the danger even of communicating with such people for fear that to be associated with him would justify the authorities in purging them from their employment. I asked him whether he could name one person who had suffered in this way, but he was unable to do so.

At the end of the interview I commenced to ask him, should he reconsider the matter and decide to inform us more fully of his past association with the Soviet Intelligence Service to notify the Governor that he desired a further interview with me, when he interrupted me to say that he had no particular reason for bearing love towards leaving MI5. His first contact with this organisation had led to ten years penal servitude as the result of the admission which he was persuaded to make to Lieut. Col. Burt. His next meeting two years ago (with Cussen and Marriott) had produced in him such a boiling rage that he found it quite impossible to discuss the case at all with them. After two years he was therefore no more pleased to see me, but he said he hoped he had not in any way appeared rude. At the time he had no wish to meet me again, and I felt that his mind was made up on this point. However, I managed to complete my instructions that he should approach the Governor should he desire to see me. He said he thought it extremely unlikely.

During the interview I made no promise or suggestion to him that any action of his would lead to a remission of sentence, although I did mention petitions which had been made from time to time by the AScW for his release. He said he was not allowed to have any knowledge of these efforts on his behalf, although in fact he was told that the AScW was currently engaged in an attempt to secure a remission of his sentence. He added that an additional reason for his dislike of my department was his transfer back to Wakefield from Leyhill. I acted complete innocence in this matter and said that it was no part of our business to arrange the transfer of prisoners, this being solely a matter for the Home Office.

I have no confidence that Nunn May will ever decide to tell his story, but there is just the outside chance that upon reflection, he will.

Skardon appears disappointed that he had not made sufficient progress, and in particular that Nunn May had not given him the name of his Russian contact. But the interview revealed one significant finding in that his recruiter was in the United Kingdom before Nunn May's departure to Canada. If he was 'well out of reach' it might mean that the person was abroad and not available for interview. They could be in the Soviet Union or any of its satellite states or even in a Russian Embassy.

Skardon suggests that the contact followed him to Canada. This would be difficult to achieve during wartime. Such a person might still be at large in North America and more alarmingly operating as a Russian agent.

Skardon appears to have adopted a relaxed, unhurried, interviewing style. Nunn May appears to have been comfortable in his company and he may have been gratified to hold an intelligent conversation with someone while being locked away in prison. It gave Nunn May an opportunity to state his loyalty to Britain, but this could not override the loyalty which he owed to his friends. Again the argument was made that the information revealed was of little value. He explicitly states that he was given great freedom of movement while in Canada and the United States. He says that he was not allowed to write up a report on his findings when he returned to the United Kingdom in 1945. He was not to know that by then, he was under surveillance and efforts were being made to limit his contact with confidential information.

He expresses his intense dislike of MI5 which he says is responsible for his plight and for his transfer back to Wakefield. His previous interrogators, Marriott and Cussen, had infuriated him, probably adopting a more censorious tone, whereas Skardon used a more affable approach and managed to get Nunn May to 'open up' more than he had previously.

Despite such a softly, softly approach, Skardon was a skilled interrogator and lost no opportunity to de-stabilise any over confidence Nunn May was feeling by suggesting that he wouldn't hesitate to approach his friends and colleagues in this matter thereby causing him some discomfort, even anguish. There is very little in the security files to follow up this interview. Nunn May undoubtedly continued to have visits from friends and family. But no letters of a personal nature to his family were now kept and recorded.

The following year in January 1950, the FBI wrote to the British Embassy in Washington, USA, raising their concerns over Nunn May's travelling arrangements while in Canada and the USA.

This followed on from the detailed Royal Commission report made into the Canadian spying scandal. There were a number of aspects which were troubling the FBI one of which was the uncertainty about the extent of Nunn May's travels while in Canada.

They managed to obtain Nunn May's travelling expense accounts. He had been to Chicago three times, and on one of those visits, remained for over a month. He also visited Toronto, and Ottawa and stopped off in New York city whilst en route to or from Chicago. The latter was at his own expense. He had visited the Atomic Plant at Chalk River, Ontario on several occasions. In September 1945, the Chalk River facility housed the first nuclear reactor to go operational outside of the USA and was followed by the closure of the Montreal Laboratory in 1946.

The FBI had been critical of what they saw as a lack of vetting by MI5 of the workers employed on the Tube Alloys Project. They were even more alarmed to learn, that Nunn May had enjoyed freedom of travel to Atomic Research Institutions in Canada and the USA. The possibility of nuclear secrets having been communicated to a person or persons unknown could be highly damaging.

In July 1950 the FBI, via the British Embassy in Washington, said that they had heard on good authority, that Nunn May had decided to fully disclose the nature of his activities on behalf of the Soviet Intelligence Services. It must have been an astonished Marriott of MI5, who immediately contacted the Governor of Wakefield Prison, to see if there had been any change in Nunn May's attitude since the Skardon interview.

The response of Guise-More, the governor was that Nunn May remained unsociable, withdrawn and introspective. He described him as an excellent prisoner who never complained and didn't grumble. He exhibited a somewhat 'holier than thou' approach and intellectual snobbishness. The governor had not received any approach by Nunn May to indicate any change of mind. He went on to say that he would speak to the prison officer who was closest to him to see if he had noticed any change of mind, but he was not hopeful of a successful outcome. The result was the same. Nunn May refused to talk about his case.

CHAPTER FOURTEEN

Nunn May's arrest and conviction had been covered by the national newspapers but the coverage had not been of the magnitude befitting someone who had passed on secrets to a foreign country. This might have been because Russia had been an ally during the war and wasn't seen as being threatening to the nation. Then in 1946, Winston Churchill delivered his 'Iron Curtain' speech in Fulton, Missouri, which ignited public consciousness to the threat from Soviet Russia. Everything changed with the onset of the Berlin Airlift in 1948 and was reinforced when in 1951, on 24 May 1951, Guy Burgess and Donald Maclean, employed by the Foreign Office defected to Russia. This event while covered in the press was underplayed by the government.

In May 1951 the *Sunday Chronicle* published an article which suggested that Nunn May and Klaus Fuchs would be released early in order to further the research which they had been allowed to undertake while in prison. Fuchs had been convicted of espionage on 1 March 1950 and sentenced to fourteen years imprisonment. He was then in prison at Stafford. The article suggested that colleagues at Harwell had studied their work and suggested that it was so important, that they should be allowed some form of controlled detention. If parole was not acceptable because of public sensibilities, this would be a more appropriate step to take. It also said that the Home Office was giving this proposal serious consideration. More tellingly the article claimed that the two men had had a change of heart concerning their political convictions.

We know that this was certainly untrue in Nunn May's case. MI5 files show that they thought the whole thing was nonsense, although a parliamentary question was placed before the Home Office which necessitated quashing any such newspaper rumours.

Interest in Nunn May's case was again evident in the press coverage. The alleged plot to engineer Nunn May's escape from prison, had uncovered animosity from certain prisoners who resented what they saw as privileges being granted to him, a convicted spy. Former inmates who had served sentences alongside Nunn May were now free to pedal their stories to journalists. In October 1951, Alan Moorehead, was given selected access to some MI5 files in connection with a publication on *'Soviet Atomic Espionage'* In January 1952, the *Sunday Express* featured an article on Nunn May's case and how he had sold secrets to the Russians whose activities were by now viewed with grave suspicion. The content of newspaper coverage was to become more damning of his spying and generated increasing anger amongst the public.

In June 1952, *The People* printed an article about how Nunn May had colluded with Douglas Springhall at Leyhill Prison. The newspaper said that the revelations must cause widespread alarm about the way dangerous traitors were guarded in our prisons. It was reported by a former inmate of Leyhill called Jamieson who had been imprisoned there for Post Office fraud.

Jamieson alleged that Springhall, who edited the prison bulletin, and Nunn May, the librarian, spent a lot of time together. Nunn May, avoided other company and often worked alone on his scientific calculations. He said that Springhall was supplied once a week with food parcels and tobacco and money which he obtained by going into a wood after dark and meeting people from the outside world. He also said that Springhall was smuggling communist propaganda into the prison via a similar route which he did on a monthly basis by meeting a dark haired foreign looking woman. Nunn May kept his work to himself but Jamieson decided that he would look at it while he was out of the way. He noted many scientific calculations which he thought the authorities including MI5 should know about. He said he was going to steal them, but decided against it, since informers were out of favour with the prison authorities. Ultimately, the two were able to keep their papers in a locked office. Jamieson went on to say that he dropped an anonymous note in the prison courtyard to alert the prison governor.

The newspaper clearly set out to alarm its readers by saying that convicted spies were still pursuing their political agendas in prison without any supervision.

We know that Nunn May was legitimately pursuing his scientific work in prison in preparation for writing a book. His former boss John Cockcroft had already commented that this work would not represent a threat to the country. The alleged remarks about the passing of items and information to inmates in an open prison was bound to raise the hackles of readers. In 1947 the authorities had alerted the police to the fact that alleged clandestine meetings were taking place outside the prison, but they reported no evidence of any irregularities. Apart from pointing out a discrepancy regarding the dates of Jamieson's story, they took no action. Perhaps it was difficult to substantiate the allegations, and the police may not have been able to devote significant time to an investigation.

Nunn May had already been transferred from Leyhill to Wakefield Prison when this was published, but again his association with Springhall, which might have given him some support at the time, was becoming a nuisance and harming his future rehabilitation. This was not to be the end of prison gossip by former inmates.

On 1 July 1952, the film director Roy Boulting of Charter Film Productions, London W1 wrote to Special Branch about a conversation with a John Hallett. Hallett had been court-martialled and sentenced at the end of the war for large scale corruption in India and Burma. He had served part of his sentence at Leyhill with Springhall and Nunn May and said that the information he had, might be exploited for the purpose of making a film. Roy Boulting thought that what he had been told seemed highly dramatic and dangerous and hence his letter.

It was Hallett's opinion that Springhall had developed a strong hold over Nunn May and reinforced his communist beliefs. Nunn May, he said was very depressed, bitter and feeling let down by his fellow scientists.

Boulting's letter was passed on to Commander Burt of Special Branch since mention had also been made of illicit handling by warders of information supplied by Klaus Fuchs in Stafford Prison. Burt commented that he thought all Hallett's remarks were speculation based on other newspaper reports and bearing in mind Hallett's long criminal record, the whole thing was nonsense. No action was taken.

The appearance of more stories about Nunn May now drew attention to his release date from prison. There had been no complaints from the prison authorities about his behaviour and therefore on the grounds of good behaviour he could be released in December 1952.

The press were certainly aware of this since it had the makings of a good story. Nunn May would become a free man, but his misdeeds were not being forgotten.

CHAPTER FIFTEEN

From July to September 1952, correspondence circulated around the Ministry of Supply (Nunn May's former employers), the Home Office, the Foreign Office and MI5 as to what should or should not be done on his release and who should be responsible for doing what. Nobody seemed too sure as to whether they could do anything or not, and the various ministries seemed at odds as to whether they needed to be involved at all.

To illustrate the dilemmas, a letter on 18 July instigated by a General Morgan, raised the issue of what actions the Ministry of Supply were going to take when Nunn May was released from prison. MFP Hockliffe at the Ministry of Supply sent the following letter to the Home Office.

> I do not know of any recognised procedure governing the disposal of a man like Alan Nunn May on his release from gaol. I presume that on his release he will be a free man.
>
> Nevertheless it is a matter to which some thought might well be given. There are two main points which should be considered and these are of interest to the Division of Atomic Energy; a) Is Nunn May in possession of information which would be of value to Russia and b) Would he himself be of value to Russia by reason of his ability as a nuclear physicist?
>
> Having obtained answers to these two points, it might then be desirable to consider what restrictions if any could be put on his movements. For example the Foreign Office might be asked to deny

him a passport, although that in itself is no bar to a determined man.

It may well be that he could give useful advice to the State in unclassified research work at, say a University. Such a post would have the advantage that he would to some extent be under the eye of some form of authority.

In any action that this department might ask the appropriate authorities to consider or not to consider, it would clearly be essential to take into consideration possible reactions from the British and American public.

You will appreciate that Nunn May was in the Tube Alloys project under the DSIR and was never actually employed by the Ministry of Supply.

I have already sought advice on some of these points and I am initiating further enquiries.

> *M.F.P. Hockliffe*
> Division of Atomic Energy
> Ministry of Supply
> Shell Mex House
> The Strand
> London WC2

This letter was to result in a flurry of activity at the Home Office and in particular MI5

The response from Martin Furnival Jones, a solicitor engaged by MI5 during wartime was that this country might wish to deny his services to Russia and try to use his skills here. Did Nunn May hold information which might be a security risk? He thought it politically undesirable for the Ministry of Supply to employ him, but he might be used as a consultant and as a trainer of nuclear physicists, and be employed by a university. An official reply on these issues would be required from the Home Office. Nunn May would be a free agent and his intentions were as yet unknown. This was something for others to find out.

Professor Perrin formerly of Tube Alloys was consulted, and said that it was unlikely Nunn May had any information which the Russians did not already possess. He also thought that his abilities as a nuclear physicist would be useful to Russia, assuming that he was willing to go there. However the same could be said of many other physicists.

The Ministry of Supply's interim statement was that it was highly improbable that they would employ Nunn May, not even in a consultancy capacity. It was possible that others (scientists) would pressurise the Ministry to engage him. A note in the files says, 'Civil Servants by training and instinct dislike answering hypothetical questions.'

By now a date for Nunn May's release from prison was set for 30 December 1952.

At this point, William Skardon was brought back into the discussions. If anyone was going to discover Nunn May's intentions, then he would be the person to do it. The Home Office pressed the Ministry of Supply asking that before Skardon saw Nunn May at Wakefield Prison, he should know whether they would assist in re-establishing Nunn May in the U.K. at, for example, a university. This might seem misguided, but for Nunn May to leave prison and immediately depart for Russia would not be good from a public relations point of view.

The Ministry of Supply's response was that they were reluctant to give any help to Nunn May. They would be quite happy if he left for Russia with his knowledge rusty. They did not want him to rebuild his nuclear physics knowledge and then go to Russia.

Roger Hollis of MI5 was to support this view. Any job in nuclear physics would eventually lead to the fringes of classified work. He also thought that the idea of young physicists being taught by a convicted Russian spy, who had not changed his views, would not be looked on favourably. If Nunn May wished to go to the Soviet Union on his release from prison, there should be no objection although Hollis thought he would not wish to go, nor would he be wanted.

During September 1952 a number of newspaper articles had appeared which asked the same questions. They knew Nunn May would be released in December and wanted to know what he was going to do. He must have hoped that the public would have quietly forgotten him, but defections, stories of other traitors and comments by former inmates forced his name back into the newspapers and generated adverse public attention.

On 12 September 1952, William Skardon visited Wakefield Prison to establish Nunn May's intentions. Initially he spoke with Mr F.C. Ransley, the new governor at Wakefield Prison.

Ransley reported that he had appointed Nunn May to be Clerk of Accounts at the prison. He had maintained observation of Nunn May's correspondence, and received reports from prison officers present when he had visitors. The consensus appeared to be, that up until a month ago, he had been confident of finding a job in the academic field on leaving prison. He had a number of influential friends and this would enable him to obtain employment as a lecturer/teacher or tutor. He also had some money in the bank and national savings certificates to tide him over for a while. He proposed, with the approval of his brother Ralph and sister in law, to stay with them at Chalfont St. Peter. He was also intending to request five days home leave (which was often granted for the purposes of rehabilitation). The governor had already made enquiries of the Prison Commission as to the likelihood of this being granted. The answer was, 'No'.

His relatives had cautioned him that there had been public condemnation of him in recent press articles and he should not be too optimistic. The newspapers had contained articles which suggested he was taking advantages of prison facilities to spread the gospel of communism. Ransley told Skardon that there was no truth in such a story. A story appeared in the *Empire News* after Nunn May's release from Wakefield Prison that he received Communist journals whilst in prison. In the House of Commons, the Tory M.P. for Altrincham and Sale, F.J. Errol, asked the Home Secretary, Sir David Maxwell Fyfe, what communist newspapers and periodicals were approved as suitable, for inmates of H.M. Prisons. Also why was this material stamped by the Crown as 'supplied for the public service'. The response was, 'According to standing orders a prisoner is allowed to have in his cell, in addition to library books, two periodicals sent in from the distributors with the seal unbroken. The standing orders do not discriminate between different classes of periodicals or between one political party or another. There is no bar to political or religious periodicals as such although it is not permissible for the headquarters of an organisation to send in propaganda unsolicited. When periodicals are received at the prison they are at once marked with the official stamp, ***Supplied for the Public Service***. There is no question of periodicals being supplied to prisoners at the public expense.'

All classes in Wakefield Prison were supervised by prison officers, and Nunn May took classes in musical appreciation. As far as Ransley was concerned, 'Nunn May's behaviour in Wakefield Prison had been impeccable'.

Skardon was to concur with the governor's opinion of how Nunn May saw his current position. He said to Nunn May that he remained interested in his past but was also interested in his future intentions. Skardon was at pains to point out that it was not the intention to hound him on his release, but it would be helpful if it was known what he was going to do. It might well help, if Skardon were to advise against applying for certain jobs. Skardon left him with his telephone number and urged him to contact him if he had a problem. Nunn May told Skardon that he was aware of the public feelings aroused in the press and he had no intention of bringing himself into conflict with the law again. He would not apply for a job at Harwell, the centre for nuclear research in the U.K. He might also be thwarted in other jobs such as at the Medical Research Council where secret methods or apparatus might be in use.

Nunn May suggested to Skardon, that because of the adverse publicity, he might change his name, but Skardon warned against concealing his identity from any future employer. Skardon said that undoubtedly the press would do their best to track him down but that this was something he would just have to face up to. A reporter, James Reid of the *Sunday Dispatch*, had already obtained access through a member of the prison staff, William Huggett, to the Prison Officer's Mess at Wakefield Prison, seeking a story about Nunn May.

Skardon felt that it had been a very constructive interview, and he concluded that Nunn May did not seem to be mentally scarred by prison, he was anxious to lead a useful life.

Certainly Nunn May had used his time in prison productively. He would not have been able to keep up to date in nuclear physics but he had continued to pursue, within the limits of prison, some work on physics. The question now would be whether he could continue with this work on release and find a suitable job, and how he might face up to adverse public opinion. He seemed to be mentally prepared for the task ahead.

During November and December of 1952, efforts were made to help Nunn May secure suitable employment after being released from prison at the end of the year.

The Wakefield Branch of The Association of Discharged Prisoners and Societies, on Nunn May's behalf, wrote to the Ministry of Labour and National Service seeking enrolment forms in order that he might be placed on their register as a scientist. Their response was to write to the Home Office seeking advice as to how they should proceed in these special circumstances. In turn that was inevitably to involve MI5 and eventually the Ministry of Supply.

In a discussion between Phillip Allen of the Home Office and Dick White of MI5, White reiterated the last conversation that had taken place between Skardon and Nunn May at Wakefield Prison on 12 September. He said that they felt it was important for Nunn May to find useful paid employment in this country. A long spell out of work might bring disillusionment and he could be tempted by offers which might conflict with national security.

Meanwhile the Government turned its attention on Nunn May's forthcoming release from prison. On 22 November 1952, the Home Secretary, David Maxwell Fyfe, prepared a memorandum for the Cabinet concerning Nunn May's release from prison. It responded to the anxiety felt by some, that if he was being granted remission on his sentence, what could be done to change it. The Home Secretary's memorandum was as follows:

> Dr Alan Nunn May was convicted at the Central Criminal Court on 1st May 1946 of communicating information contrary to the Official Secrets Act and was sentenced to 10 years imprisonment. Under the prison rules a prisoner may earn the remission of up to one third of his sentence by good conduct and industry. Nunn May's behaviour has been good and he has earned the maximum remission. Provided he continues to behave well, he will become due for discharge on 29th

December 1952. Discharge will be unconditional.

It has been suggested that Nunn May's release will give rise to public anxiety in this country and to unfavourable comment in the United States and Canada and that it would therefore be right to withhold the remission which he has earned and detain him until his sentence expires in 1956.

It is true, that in law, a prisoner could be detained until the expiration of his sentence and could not claim damages for wrongful imprisonment if he were so detained, but in practice, if a prisoner does not forfeit any remission by misconduct, he is released automatically after he has served two thirds of his sentence without any reference to the Prison Commissioners or the Secretary of State. The Prison Rules, which are statutory instruments submitted to Parliament contemplate that a prisoner will be able to earn remission of up to one third of his sentence by good conduct and industry, and a prisoner naturally assumes that, if he behaves well, he will be able to earn the normal remission and will only serve two-thirds of his sentence. Indeed a card posted up in his cell informs him to this effect. The terms of the Prison Rules are well known, and the court, in fixing what is regarded as an appropriate sentence of ten years imprisonment, had in mind that Nunn May would, subject to good conduct, be released after serving six years and eight months. The fact that he will be due for discharge at the end of December was mentioned in the Press some time ago and is therefore, common knowledge. To deprive him at the last moment of the fruits of his good behaviour, when throughout his sentence he has been led to believe that he could earn the normal remission of sentence, would be open to criticism on the ground that it was arbitrary and unjust, and involved a gross breach of faith. No comparable action has been taken in any case for at least forty years.

I recognise that Nunn May's release must inevitably give cause for anxiety. His information may no longer be up to date, but his abilities remain, and when he is released, there will be no power under which he could be prevented from leaving this country and going to any other country which might wish to use his services. He could not, however in any event be detained beyond 30 April 1956, and in my view, the risks attendant on his release are likely to be less if he is released in the normal course, than if the exceptional course were taken of detaining him until the end of his sentence and then releasing him in an inevitably embittered state of mind. This is a judgement on the psychological probabilities based on the views which those who have seen him in prison have formed. I am not technically qualified to assess how important his knowledge would be now or how much less important it would be in three years time.

No doubt Nunn May's release will receive much publicity in the Press and it may be that it will be criticised in the United States and it is unfortunate that his release date should be reached at a time when we have some hope of persuading the Americans to exchange information about atomic secrets. Under the United States federal law however, any prisoner serving more that one year may be released on parole when he has served only one third of his sentence.

For the reasons I have given, I do not consider that it would be right to deprive Nunn May of the remission of sentence which he has earned by good conduct, but I have thought it right to bring the matter to the notice of my colleagues.

Sir David Maxwell Fyfe, Q.C., M.P.
Secretary of State for the Home Department and
Minister for Welsh Affairs
22nd November 1952

In making his statement, Maxwell Fyfe was able to call upon information from MI5, and provide the legal position. He was also aware of American sensitivities and the need to remain on good terms with them. This was a recurring theme, and would continue to resurface for some years.

Maxwell Fyfe's memorandum was put forward as an agenda item at a meeting of the Cabinet on 25 November 1952. The Prime Minister, Winston Churchill, was in the Chair.

Among the points raised was that the Judge in passing sentence of ten years would know that Nunn May could earn remission of one third of that sentence.

Who would employ a man like Nunn May who had committed treachery against the State? He could not be employed in Government service nor by any firm involved with the defence industry. Perhaps some scientists who were friends, might find him employment.

His knowledge of atomic energy was out of date and it was unlikely that he could provide information to a potential enemy. However, if after release he made his way to the Soviet Union, there would be a public outcry which would impair Anglo American co-operation on atomic energy.

The general view of the Cabinet was that before Nunn May was released, ways should be sought of preventing him leaving the country until the full ten years of his sentence had expired. They asked the Home Secretary to find out before his release, whether any assurances might be forthcoming from Nunn May that he would not leave the country during that period, whether he had a home and family to return to, and his prospects of employment.

On 10 December 1952, Maxwell Fyfe, produced another memorandum in response to a request by Cabinet. He spent a significant amount of time in explaining the legal options of attempting to detain Nunn May in the UK. His memorandum was as follows:

> The Criminal Justice Act 1948 abolished the old ticket of leave system when penal servitude was abolished and there is now no power to release Nunn May on licence.
>
> Other ways of releasing him subject to the following conditions a) that he should not leave the United Kingdom and b) if he attempted to do so he should be liable to recall to prison to complete his sentence.

Maxwell Fyfe then went on to describe as to how this might be achieved.

Release on parole under Rule 84 of the Prison Rules. This was open to objections of principle and law.
  i) Section 47 (5) of the Prison Act 1952, replaced the rule making power in the Criminal Justice Act 1948, provides that Rules,

"may provide for the temporary release of persons serving a sentence of imprisonment" and the Rule provides that a prisoner "may be temporarily absent from prison on parole for a stated length of time".

ii) Thus the statutory provisions clearly contemplate that the prisoner should return to prison after a period of parole and it should be inconsistent with their obvious intention to release a prisoner on parole for the whole of the unexpired term of his sentence.

iii) I have considered whether it would be possible to free him for a number of successive "stated lengths of time" (say six months), on these conditions. For such a course to be of any value it would have to be made clear to Nunn May that if he kept the conditions he would be free for the remainder of his sentence. This makes such a course highly artificial even if it were legally valid.

Conditional Pardon

This is also open to objections.

i) In the eyes of the man in the street such a course would involve the Queen giving special treatment to a traitor.

ii) To use a conditional pardon to impose conditions on the release of a prisoner who has earned the ordinary remission on his sentence, is a subterfuge to reintroduce the ticket of leave system which Parliament has abolished.

iii) It would be wrong to use the Prerogative of Mercy not to ameliorate a prisoner's lot but to make him worse off than other prisoners in a similar position.

iv) The main use of Conditional Pardon is to commute the death sentence to life imprisonment. This practice is governed by statute. There is a common law power to attach any other conditions to the grant of a pardon in other cases, but it has seldom been used, and is generally to substitute one form of sentence for another e.g. detention in an approved school for detention in a Borstal institution or a fine for imprisonment. No use has ever been made of this power to impose a condition which did not at the

same time confer a benefit on the prisoner.
v) Where there is no statutory sanction for the grant of a Conditional Pardon, the condition must not only be reasonable and capable of performance by the prisoner but also be accepted by him
vi) If Nunn May accepted the condition, and was released, but subsequently broke the condition, it might be difficult to enforce it. If such a condition is broken the Pardon ceases to have any effect, and the position quo ante revives. There have been a few cases where this view has been acted on e.g. one where a young man broke a condition that he should go to a training school and remain there until the end of his sentence and the police were then asked to arrest him and he was returned to Borstal to complete his original sentence. If a conditional pardon were granted to Nunn May, it might afford sufficient authority to instruct the police at all ports to arrest him if he attempted to leave the country. But if he were arrested and returned to prison in these circumstances, the action taken would be likely to arouse very strong criticism.

In a memorandum to his Cabinet colleagues, Maxwell Fyfe had examined the possible legal options but rejected them as a means by which Nunn May could be prevented from leaving the country. He went on to say that it would be wrong to deprive Nunn May of the remission he had earned and so to require him to serve the full ten years of his sentence. He then expresses his own views on Nunn May's future in his final paragraph.

The risks attendant on Nunn May's release are likely to be less if he is released in the normal course than if the exceptional course of detaining him until the end of his sentence were taken. I understand that those who have seen him in prison, although they cannot speak with certainty of his present beliefs or state of mind, have formed the impression that, if suitable work could be found for him, he would probably settle down quietly in England and would not seek to leave this country and put his services at the disposal of any foreign power. He is not married and I understand that he intends to stay with his brother on his release. Special efforts would be made to find him appropriate employment and I am advised that there are several fields in which it may be possible to do so without prejudice to security. If however he were detained for the full ten years he would be likely to have a considerable sense of grievance when he was eventually discharged, and would be less likely to remain in this country.

Thus Maxwell Fyfe while giving legal opinions on the matter, also took into account the views of officers in MI5, notably Jim Skardon. He was also setting out an initiative to secure Nunn May employment which would require a great deal of time and effort from different parts of the Whitehall political apparatus.

Maxwell Fyfe presented this second memorandum to a meeting of the Cabinet on 16 December 1952, again with the Prime Minister, Winston Churchill in the Chair.

Maxwell Fyfe reiterated his findings to the Cabinet in that there were no legal reasons to prevent Nunn May from leaving the country when he was released and that he thought he should be released on the date which took account of his remission.

Winston Churchill said that he appreciated the Home Secretary's difficulty, but Nunn May's release would excite public interest and strong dissatisfaction would be felt if he went abroad soon afterwards. "There will be trouble. I would keep him for the whole term but … He should be kept under close supervision by the Police."

The Marquess of Reading, Joint Parliamentary Under Secretary of State, Foreign Office, said that they proposed to inform the United States Government in advance of May's impending release, and to provide the British authorities in the United States with suitable information and guidance to enable them to deal with any enquiries from the American Press.

The Cabinet:
    1. Agreed that Alan Nunn May should be released from prison on the date when he would ordinarily be due for

discharge by reason of the remission which he had earned by good conduct and industry during his imprisonment.
2. Took note with approval of the arrangements proposed for dealing with any unfavourable comment which his release might arouse in the United States.

CHAPTER SIXTEEN

The Home Office continued its efforts to find Nunn May employment. Dick White of MI5, also asked the Home Office if appealing to the press not to hound Nunn May might be a good idea, since again this might push him towards unwanted liaisons.

The Ministry of Supply contacted their Division of Atomic Energy and their response as regards work in this field was, not surprisingly, that it was out of the question. They did however agree to contacting John Cockcroft, Nunn May's former boss to seek his advice on the matter.

An organisation called the Central After Care Association (CACA) had contacted a number of companies on Nunn May's behalf but the replies were unhelpful. They included Ferranti in Lancashire who were doing government work, much of which was secret. The Medical Research Council had no vacancies; British Rayon Research in Manchester said he would have to call on them, but change his name; Gabbitas Thring of London, said that enrolment on a list for teaching posts would be useless.

Nunn May's brother Ralph had contacted Nunn May's trade union the AScW to see if they could help. A member of staff, Ben Smith, arranged to meet Revd Martin Pinker of CACA and Nunn May at Wakefield. MI5 seemed to monitor the AScW's activities and ensured that the meeting was 'tactfully' supervised.

Nunn May had also been approached by Elek Books of Great James St., London WC2 to write his life story. He did consider the offer seriously, and of course it would provide an income. He was advised by the Home Office and MI5, that this would be inappropriate since this could jeopardise any hope of securing long term employment. In any case, any mention of his work at Tube Alloys was still subject to the Official Secrets Act. Nunn May did engage in correspondence with them but did not pursue the idea.

John Cockcroft proved very helpful in setting out a number of possibilities for Nunn May which the Ministry of Supply forwarded to the Home Office. They were:

> A teacher of physics. He had spent most of his life since graduation in teaching and research. There was an acute shortage of physics teachers in schools.
> A hospital physicist in departments of biophysics or radiotherapy. He would be an expert in the theory of such work. Cockcroft thought this to be the best option.
> There was also work in the industrial field of advanced physical instrumentation, the application of radiation, Xrays and gamma rays.

There were to be no firm offers of employment, a fact which would not have surprised Nunn May. He would soon be released from prison and again the press had the story.

The *Sunday Chronicle* said his date of release would be Saturday 27 December 1952. They said, 'Two leap years in jail mean his release would be on Sunday 28 December, but as no prisoner is ever released on a Sunday the Prison Commissioners have decided to let him go on the day before'. The date quoted was incorrect.

The news of Nunn May's release was being assimilated in the United States. There had been considerable unease since Nunn May's trial and other trials which had taken place in the interim – Klaus Fuchs in particular – that vetting of those engaged by the British Government on secret work was unsatisfactory. They were alarmed at the possibility of Soviet Agents infiltrating the British Intelligence services, a concern which had been amplified by the defection of Burgess and MacLean in

1951. The trial in the USA of Julius and Ethel Rosenberg, convicted of spying and espionage had taken place and they were due to be executed in January 1953. The fact that a former British spy for the Soviets i.e. Nunn May, had been given a remission on his sentence, and there were to be no restrictions on his freedom, was a source of extreme irritation. This was a time of collaboration and sharing of information on the development of nuclear weapons between the British and the Americans. The British Government were acutely aware that this should not be jeopardised by what the Americans saw as security lapses and the continuation of a a lax approach.

The Foreign Office in collaboration with the Home Office spent a great deal of time drafting and redrafting carefully worded press statements and endeavoured to explain to the Americans, through our Embassy in Washington, why Nunn May's imminent release was confined by current laws in the U.K. An extract of correspondence from the British Embassy in Washington to the Foreign Office, reveals the disquiet:

> Our respect for the law would earn us no credit from the Americans and might well invite objections which it would be very difficult for us to ignore without serious damage to our relations and to the prospects of future cooperation. They are at the moment in an hysterical state about disloyalty and their actions show how little they themselves are inhibited by legal considerations when their own security is concerned. Even if they accepted our argument that we are legally debarred from taking action, they would be quite unable to understand why the necessary legislation should not be introduced.
>
> In general the whole position could hardly be more unsatisfactory. As soon as we get over one security incident another arises...

The issue focused on the possibility of Nunn May leaving the country although he had already indicated that he would not do this. The Foreign Office in their correspondence to the British Embassy in Washington said:

> Unfortunately there are no means of releasing the prisoner

conditionally. The Criminal Justice Act 1948 abolished the old ticket of leave system when penal servitude was abolished and there is now no power to release Nunn May on licence ... The Home Secretary has considered whether any other way of releasing him subject to conditions can be found. He has been unable to find any means by which Nunn May could be effectively be prevented from leaving this country after his release if he wishes to do so. It would be quite impracticable to introduce special legislation to deal with an individual case. This is the position and we cannot get away from it.

Nunn May did not hold a passport. The question of Nunn May leaving the UK with or without a passport was considered at some length. The Foreign Office were advised that it was not a legal necessity in peace time, under United Kingdom law at present in force, for a British subject to be in possession of a valid passport, although in practice, foreign countries or travel companies insisted on valid documents. It was established practice that passports were only refused to British subjects in well defined categories. The only one which fitted these circumstances was, 'where the activities of an individual are so notoriously undesirable or dangerous that Parliament would be expected to support this action of the Secretary of State in refusing or confiscating a passport'.

CHAPTER SEVENTEEN

On Monday 29 December 1952 Alan Nunn May was released from Wakefield Prison after being arrested and taken into custody on 4 March 1946 and convicted at his trial on 1 May 1946. He was escorted from the prison at 3 a.m. by a squad car to Doncaster where he met his sister in law Jackie, before travelling by train to King's Cross and then on to Chalfont St. Peter.

He went to live with his brother Ralph and his wife Jackie at Beech Cottage, High Street, Chalfont St. Peter, Buckinghamshire.

On 30 December 1952, the day after Nunn May's release from Wakefield Prison, there was another Cabinet meeting. On one of the agenda items, the Foreign Secretary, Anthony Eden, raised the issue of Nunn May being granted a passport. He said, that he had the discretion to refuse or confiscate a passport in certain classes of case including those very rare cases where the activities of an individual were so notoriously undesirable or dangerous that Parliament could be expected to uphold his action in doing so. He considered this such a case and said that if May asked for a passport his request should be rejected.

Maxwell Fyfe supported this view and the decision was approved by the Cabinet. The ramifications of this decision and the reasoning behind it would rumble on for some time.

On 30 December Alan Nunn May provided the following statement to the Press Association:

I do not wish to discuss the details of the action which led to my imprisonment. I myself think that I acted rightly and I believe many others think so too.

To those who think otherwise I would like to point out that I have suffered the punishment which was inflicted on me by the law and I hope I shall now be entitled to at least the consideration normally granted to released convicts: an opportunity to restart life.

There is just one of many erroneous statements of fact which I should like to correct now. I was not convicted of treason nor was this word used by the prosecution or judge at my trial and I certainly had no treasonable intentions.

I was wholeheartedly concerned with procuring victory over Nazi Germany. My object now is to obtain as soon as possible an opportunity of doing useful scientific work in which I can be of some service to the country and to my fellow men.

Now that my imprisonment is over I can only wish for the same consideration and fair treatment which I received throughout the long period of my sentence from the prison officials and my fellow prisoners.

Signed *AN May*

No further statement will be made or interviews given.

Nunn May's release from Wakefield Prison was widely reported in the national press. A number of newspapers took the opportunity to comment on his actions in their leader columns. The *Daily Express* said in its Opinion column that 'some scientists had shown woolly minded sympathy towards Nunn May rather than sympathy for the country he had betrayed. Although he has served his sentence he had not earned society's forgiveness.'

Another newspaper picked up on his press statement, 'I myself think that I acted rightly and I believe many others think so too'. It said, 'this demonstrated a forthright declaration of impenitence which has grave implications. Nunn May displayed moral arrogance in 1945 and he was still blind to it now. There was a danger that this would afflict other brilliant misguided scientists. Security in nuclear research must never relax.'

On 31 December 1952, arrangements were made for a watch on all incoming and outgoing letters from Nunn May's residence at Chalfont St. Peter. A meeting was arranged with the Chief Constable of Buckinghamshire, Colonel T.R.P. Warren. They were asked to provide any indication which might come to hand that Nunn May was leaving his current address for anything more than a temporary visit. The point was emphasised that in no way should Nunn May be hounded, since steps were being taken to secure him employment and there was no wish to drive him into a desperate act, such as leaving the country.

They were also asked to be sympathetic to requests for assistance from Nunn May or his brother, if he received abusive letters or unwelcome callers at the house. The address had been published in the press. Any enquiries instigated by the police should be tactful and discreet. It transpired that Special Branch had a good informant in the village. There was no separate telephone line to link the constabulary with MI5 and it was agreed that messages relayed from the constabulary would use a code name for Nunn May … Mrs Norma Martin.

So Alan Nunn May was to change sex as well!

The Home Office together with MI5 agreed that instructions should be sent to all Immigration and Special Branch officers at ports regarding action to be taken if Nunn May tried leaving the country. It was stressed that no powers existed to prevent him from doing so, but no doubt some reason could be found to delay him while MI5 were informed.

On 1 January 1953, William Skardon wrote to Nunn May suggesting that they meet up to discuss his future, including the subject of suitable employment. He said that he fully understood if he wanted to meet away from Chalfont St. Peter, because of press intrusion.

Nunn May replied by letter on 2 January to Skardon, who had given his address as Room 055 at the War Office in Whitehall. He said he had an appointment at the Ministry of Labour on 7 January at 10:30 a.m. and if it was convenient he could call on Skardon that day. If the 6 January was more convenient he could come to the house in Chalfont St. Peter since there had been no signs of any press for the last two days.

The letter was written in quite friendly terms and it seemed that Skardon was a man whom Nunn May could happily converse with and felt might also be useful to him. The situation seemed to be calming down until a telephone call was received by the Sunday *Empire News*.

On Thursday 1 January 1953 an Irish freelance journalist called John McGrath had offered that newspaper a story that Nunn May was proceeding to Eire on Saturday 3 January and this was the first step before going to Argentina to work there on an atomic project. McGrath had visited the Argentine Ambassador in London along with a reporter Ernest Bennett from the Sunday *Empire News* and said that the Argentinians were enthusiastic about it. Bennett was not present at this meeting. McGrath said he was a friend of Ralph Nunn May and he also knew Alan Nunn May. McGrath had been in touch with them and had booked two seats on an Aer Lingus plane due to leave Northolt Airport for Dublin at 3 p.m. on Saturday 3 January. The seats were booked in McGrath's name. The newspaper checked that this was indeed the case.

McGrath said that Nunn May would be prepared to write one article for the newspaper as a sort of final broadside before he departed. McGrath claimed to have written Nunn May's press statement, except the passage in which he said he had acted correctly.

A reliable and well placed informer passed on this information to MI6 and it was relayed onwards to the Home Office and thence MI5. The informer also commented that McGrath was not a reliable source.

On Friday 2 January at 6 p.m., the security services, after some enquiries, received information from a contact at British European Airways. The District Traffic Superintendent of Aer Lingus at Dorland Hall had told him that a John McGrath and Dr Nunn May plus a third passenger whose name would be supplied later, were booked on Flight No 149 to Dublin, leaving Northolt at 3:20 p.m. on Saturday 3 January. The Traffic Superintendent had been approached directly by McGrath who said these bookings were confidential and he must not reveal the names to anyone. The Traffic Superintendent noticed the name of Nunn May and was perturbed that this might bring about unwelcome publicity to the airline. He telephoned Dublin for advice but was unable to contact anyone so he gave the story to the Irish Consulate in London. They in turn contacted a government department in Dublin.

With this information to hand MI5 acted quickly. William Skardon accompanied by a colleague, proceeded to Beech Cottage, 6 High Street, Chalfont St. Peter, the home of Ralph Nunn May, where Alan had been residing since his release from Wakefield Prison. Skardon arrived there alone at 7:40 p.m. that same evening.

He was received by Ralph Nunn May's wife Jackie and explained that he was an officer in the Security Service. She was reluctant to believe this, but eventually allowed him into the house where he met her husband, Ralph, and Alan Nunn May.

Skardon explained that the reason for his visit was that there was a persistent press rumour that Alan Nunn May was leaving the country tomorrow Saturday 3 January. Nunn May denied this vehemently. The first he had known about it was in a letter which had been sent express post and had just been delivered ten minutes before Skardon's arrival. The hand written letter dated 2 January written on notepaper from the Savoy Hotel, London, was sent to Alan Nunn May by John McGrath. The letter said:

Dear Dr Nunn May

I have greatly admired your courageous and disciplined attitude and restraint.

It seems to me that while you are resting and planning the future the best retreat for you would be Ireland. My aunt in Carlow would be delighted to entertain you and your presence there would be unnoticed.

I am flying over tomorrow and if you wish you could come with me or join me later.

I am sending this message by express post to you. As you are not on the phone I will if I may call in on you this evening about 7.30pm.

Yours sincerely
John McGrath

The time was now 8 p.m., Friday 2 January and there was no sign of McGrath. What on earth was Skardon doing there. Was this some sort of plot concocted by MI5 to ensnare Alan Nunn May using a bogus message? His brother and sister in law voiced their suspicions about Skardon and they both remained sceptical of him and his motives. Alan Nunn May seemed unaffected by the whole thing. Skardon decided that he needed his colleague to back him up. Skardon in the company of Ralph Nunn May went to a nearby hotel to collect his colleague who was able to confirm Skardon's story. Suspicions were difficult to allay, and after accepting some refreshment the conversation became easier. Skardon became convinced that Nunn May had not changed his mind about settling down and to earning his living in the U.K. He was troubled that his press statement had been misunderstood and misrepresented. He wished to be allowed to settle down quietly and had no intention of doing wrong. Skardon remarked afterwards that Nunn May's sister in law had a strong personality and appeared anxious to ensure that Alan would not go overseas and would remain under her wing. She and her husband Ralph (a member of the local Conservative Association) were loyal citizens of the UK. The interview terminated at 10:30 p.m. and ended more harmoniously than it had begun. Skardon and his colleague departed.

It had been a challenging evening for the Nunn May family and then at 1 a.m. on the morning of Saturday 3 January, just three hours later, there was a knock at their door. It was a gentleman aged about thirty, five feet ten inches tall with blue eyes who introduced himself as Major McGrath accompanied by a journalist Ernest Bennett. McGrath entered the house alone but the Nunn Mays' must have been taken aback by what happened next.

McGrath apologised for the lateness of the hour saying that his car had broken down. He said he had an office in Fleet Street, and was on friendly terms with leading members of the press. He had been educated at Stoneyhurst where he had lost his Irish accent. His actual business was making gramophone recordings of weddings for sale to the bride and groom. McGrath set about persuading Nunn May to accept the hospitality of his aunt's house in Eire. He was not aggressive in doing so, and was quite relaxed in his approach. Alan responded by saying he had no intention of accepting such an invitation to Eire or anywhere else under his auspices. The family challenged him about arranging flights to Eire in advance of any agreement having taken place. McGrath denied that he had arranged flights for Nunn May, he had only done so for himself. Undeterred he remained until 3 a.m. recanting various tales and stories which appeared to amuse the Nunn Mays. On leaving, he said he would call again later at about 10:30 a.m. to see if Nunn May had changed his mind.

By 10:30 a.m. on Saturday 3 January, McGrath had not appeared, and Ralph's wife telephoned Skardon with an account of their conversation with him. At the same time information came to the security services that no further developments had taken place overnight and Aer Lingus had received no advice from their Head Office in Dublin. McGrath was supposed to have collected the tickets at 5:30 p.m. on 2 January but did not do so. Aer Lingus cancelled the booking at 12 noon on Saturday 3 January but noted that there was plenty of room on the plane if somebody arrived at the last minute. Aer Lingus then telephoned to say that McGrath had cancelled the booking that day at 2:10p.m.

It transpired that the Sunday *Empire News* did not print the story and they refused to pay McGrath anything. He had also approached the *Sunday Dispatch* on Saturday evening, offering an interview with Nunn May for the sum of twenty five pounds. They declined his offer. A story headed *'Nunn May turns down Peron offer'* was printed on Friday 9 January in the *Daily Express* but received only minor coverage. The security services viewed McGrath's actions as a stunt to gain him self money and recognition.

On 3 January a message was dispatched from the Foreign Office to the British Embassy in Washington informing them of McGrath's approach to Nunn May. It said that Nunn May would not be departing for Ireland and that having spoken to him had been assured that he would remain in the U.K. It was important to pass on this knowledge in case a story should appear in the newspapers reporting that Nunn May was fleeing the country. This would arouse bad feelings in the USA where the Rosenburgs were appealing against their death sentence for spying. The British attitude to its convicted spies was seen by many

American politicians and the press as lenient and feeble. The Foreign Office was also able to say that any application by Nunn May for a passport would be refused. This information was secret. Any questions from the press would be met by saying that if he applied for a passport it would be considered at the time.

Winston Churchill was due to visit the USA and might have to answer awkward questions. The urgency with which the Foreign Office responded to this incident indicates the sensitivity they attached to security surrounding Nunn May, and the continuing need to reassure the USA that they were in control of the situation.

As had previously been arranged, Skardon went to meet Alan Nunn May on Tuesday 6 January 1953 at Beech Cottage. The prime purpose was to prepare for Nunn May's meeting with the Ministry of Labour on the next day, and to extend help to the Nunn Mays in future. At the Ministry he would be interviewed by two people, one an Under Secretary and a scientist, with a view to seeking appropriate employment. It was not their intention to go over his past history. He had said he was anxious to make a fresh start and to settle down. The question of his changing his name was raised again but it was felt this would not be helpful and would merely lead to accusations of deception, which he wished to avoid.

Skardon also discussed with the Nunn Mays as to how he, Skardon, and the local police could assist with unwanted intrusions into their private lives, which might occur for some considerable time. He had already laid on arrangements for assistance from the Buckinghamshire Constabulary. A Detective Inspector Fewtrell from Chesham Police Station had been appointed to liaise with them, and he had already made a favourable impression with the Nunn Mays'. The family were also trying to get a telephone installed but were on a waiting list. Skardon asked if he might intervene on their part to get it installed as soon as possible and they readily agreed. Although press intervention had caused the security services some alarm, its irritation to the family had provided MI5 with a legitimate reason for helping them and in so doing gain their confidence. Whether they knew it or not covert surveillance was to continue. The meeting had gone well, and Skardon treated the Nunn Mays' to lunch at the Bull Hotel, Gerrards Cross. He dropped them off afterwards at Ralph Nunn May's studios at Beaconsfield.

The next day, Wednesday 7 January 1953, Alan Nunn May met with a Professor Wardlow, a Mr Cantelo and a Col. A. Kearn at the Ministry of Labour. Nunn May said that he wanted to concentrate on finding employment in the U.K. He realised the difficulties he faced but appeared cheerful, intellectually vigorous and was able to see the funny side of the McGrath incident. He had assumed that a university post was impossible, but was willing to consider anything in this direction. He thought that medical research might be a promising line but he had not approached anyone nor had he been approached. He had received offers from the press to write for them, but had refused. He might agree to a small amount of writing and reviewing anonymously. He was prepared to give the interview panel a free hand. The question of a change of name was raised once more but was rejected for the time being.

If Nunn May had bought the *Daily Sketch* that day he would have been confronted with news of his former colleague at Bristol University, Professor C.F. Powell. He was also a physicist, whose lecture tour in Germany had just been cancelled by the Foreign Office at twelve hours notice. Powell was a Nobel Prize winner in 1950 and was also acquainted with Klaus Fuchs. He had visited Nunn May and collaborated on a scientific paper at Leyhill Prison and at Wakefield Prison. Powell commented that the Foreign Office were uneasy about his political affiliations although he thought they had panicked.

The article was picked up by Victor Feather who was then Assistant Secretary of the T.U.C. Feather was considered to be well informed on Communist penetration of trades unions. He noted that Powell and Guy Burgess were contemporaries at Bristol (Burgess worked for the BBC); Powell visited Nunn May in prison; Powell was in Canada when Burgess was in Washington. He informed the Home Office of his suspicions and was thanked by them. They would 'look into it'.

As far as the Americans were concerned and in particular their

Atomic Energy Commission, the current status of Nunn May remained a concern. The Americans were determined to get some answers, to what for them, were serious issues. On 5 January 1953, a member of the British Embassy in Washington was called to the State Department and was asked to provide answers to questions submitted by the Atomic Energy Commission concerning Nunn May's situation. Those questions were:

> Will he be granted a passport?
> Will he be under surveillance?
> Does the British Government know what his plans are to earn a living?

The reason given for the enquiry was that the Atomic Energy Commission of the United States was working closely with their British counterparts and it seemed reasonable that for this cooperation to continue, they should be in possession of the British Government's intentions regarding Nunn May. It was pointed out that they were being pressurised by the Joint Committee and individual congressmen who wanted answers to these questions.

At the meeting the British response was to say that no decision had been taken as to whether or not a passport would be issued since he had not asked for one. If he applied the Foreign Secretary would give his decision based on what Nunn May intended to do.

We know that a decision had already been taken to refuse such a request but the Americans were not told about this. The reasoning was that if Nunn May knew about it, he might choose to leave in a clandestine way since the lack of a passport did not of itself prevent him from leaving the country. As regards employment, the British said that Nunn May had been interviewed by the Security Service and had told them that he intended to make an honest living and had no intention of leaving the country. They did not tell the Americans that he was under surveillance. In a report of this meeting to the Foreign Office, Kit Steel of the British Embassy skated very carefully over what might be stated in a communication to the United States State Department. The final paragraph of Steel's letter to the Foreign Office reads:

> Although we probably have the material with which to answer them, in view of the delicate nature of the case I should like to be told exactly what should be said, preferably in the form of a text which could be communicated to the State Department. Since the danger of leakage from Congress is very real, I realise that this memorandum cannot be very explicit. I would therefore suggest that in addition rather than tell the Secretary of State personally and in confidence, the FBI should be given the facts orally and that Patterson should ask them to do their best to reassure the Atomic Energy Commission without divulging them. Patterson thinks the FBI can be trusted.

The Foreign Office, in a letter to Furnival-Jones at MI5 requesting comments, said that any official text sent to the Americans must be very guarded in its content. They remarked that it would do no harm to say something more about Nunn May's job prospects and mention the 'reported' job offer from Argentina. The possibility of informing the FBI was rebuffed. The final decision as to what should or should not be included in any text is perhaps summed up by the final paragraph of this letter.

> Finally there is, I think, a hint which might be made orally to the State Department when the text is handed over and that is that while the arguments put forward may not seem very convincing to American minds, our security people have their own methods which they too are not prepared to disclose.

Thus the text to be viewed by the Americans would contain little that was new about Nunn May.

CHAPTER EIGHTEEN

The surveillance of Nunn May at Chalfont St. Peter was ongoing. It was explained to Detective Sergeants Secker and Bowker of the Buckinghamshire Constabulary that they should note any unusual movements and that Immigration Officers at all ports had been notified. The latter had been asked to inform the Home Office immediately in an attempt to delay him, although, even without a passport, there was little they could do if he insisted on leaving.

It was decided that the police should be as discreet as possible. A good relationship had been established with the Nunn May family and this must not be compromised. The police had already been in touch with several people who had agreed to assist them in their task. They included an ex-police constable who lived opposite the Nunn Mays', an estate agent and magistrate whose office was next door to the Nunn Mays', the local taxi driver and the Station Master at Gerrards Cross. On 29 January 1953, a telephone tap was ordered on Gerrards Cross 3644, the line recently installed in the Nunn May house.

The question of Nunn May's future employment continued to exercise the minds of government officials. Initial lines of enquiry via the Ministry of Labour had drawn a blank. Nunn May reiterated that he was willing to consider all suggestions and had an open mind as to where the job might be located. The government and in particular MI5, were keen to bring about a solution to the problem, although this would necessitate bringing pressure to bear on sceptical prospective employers. Solving this problem would require a co-ordinated and concerted effort between different government departments each of whom had their own agenda to pursue. It was not an easy task. It would also necessitate contacting highly placed individuals in various organisations and institutions for their help, whilst bearing in mind the sensitivity attached to appointing someone with Nunn May's history. Nunn May had indicated his willingness to consider all reasonable offers, but it was highly unlikely that he would be allowed to do anything remotely connected with nuclear physics and other scientific work might be too remote from his experience. The line of persuasion was that if the U.K. could not provide Nunn May with employment, he would become disillusioned and be attracted by offers from other countries of the wrong political persuasion. The next six months were to involve much discussion and procrastination.

As regards earning some money Nunn May had submitted two articles to *Answers* magazine of Amalgamated Press, Farringdon Street, London EC4 for which he had received twelve guineas per article. The editor, Norman Edwards, asked he if he would do more on the lines of a column entitled '*Ask the Professor*'. One was to be called *What Is The Sound Barrier*, and another '*Man And Speed. Is There A Limit?*' This was a help but would not last for long.

The Home Office proposed that Nunn May might be engaged by a Correspondence Teaching College since this would get around the personnel difficulties of being involved with other staff. Nunn May suggested that he might edit scientific papers for the Ministry of Supply. It was often necessary to examine all published work on a particular subject in order to prepare a précis for an envisaged research project. This came to nothing.

The Ministry of Labour then approached William Lawrence Bragg. He was a physicist who had been appointed to be the Director of the Cavendish Laboratory after World War II, and had been awarded a Nobel Prize in 1915. He in turn contacted Sir William Ogg, Director of Rothamsted Horticultural Experimental Station. Ogg responded that there was an ongoing project on trace elements in soil, but was not enthusiastic about the idea of employing Nunn May. He straightaway raised his concerns on the propagation of communist ideas to his staff. It would require the agreement of the Ministry of Agriculture and Fisheries to whom they were attached, as well as support from the Home Office. Sir William Slater, Secretary of the Agricultural Research Council then became involved. He put forward another proposal in place of Rothamsted. He thought that a study being undertaken on radioactive elements in soil at Long Ashton near Bristol would be more suitable.

It was then the turn of Lord Rothschild, Chairman of the Agricultural Research Council to become involved. Victor Rothschild had worked in MI5 during the war, he was an eminent scientist and was acquainted with distinguished figures in all parts of society. He and Bragg conferred and decided that Rothamsted was not a satisfactory establishment for Nunn May and proposed two different options. One of these was the Agricultural Research Council Unit of Soil Physics at Cambridge under Dr E.C. Childs. They were studying the diffusion of water through soil, the mathematics of which was beyond agriculturalists. It might also involve electronic and physical measurements. The second option was with the Macauley Institute at Aberdeen. The work there involved emission spectroscopy and other measuring devices.

Meanwhile, Sir William Slater wrote to Guy Liddell at MI5 confirming his resistance to a job at Rothamsted being offered unless it really was in the national interest, and the Foreign Office were willing to apply leverage to the Ministry of Agriculture and Fisheries.

Nunn May was interviewed by a Dr Hartley from the Pest Control Research Department at the Macauley Institute, and the interview went well. There was however no Physics Division at Pest Control although they were keen to set one up and they would be agreeable to Nunn May to running it. This initially seemed very hopeful but the Governing Body of the Macauley Institute turned down the proposal and it appeared that Rothamsted would have to be reconsidered.

The Ministry of Labour then secured him an appointment with an industrial concern in Cambridge. The firm had requested that their identity be withheld for the time being but Nunn May agreed to be interviewed by them. The firm in question was Pye Radio. It transpired at interview, that they were willing to set him up in a laboratory based in London to do fundamental research on their behalf and pay him £1,000 per annum. Nunn May was then interviewed by the Ministry of Labour and he asked them if there would be any security issues, if he accepted such an offer. This idea seemed to be very promising. They referred to a Dr Wooster who had his own laboratory in Cambridge and worked for Pye Radio under similar conditions. Two directors of Pye contacted the Ministry of Supply about their proposal and they in turn sought advice from their own scientists as to whether this job might impinge on defence secrets. They expressed the view that this work was connected with colour television, the development of transistors and that aspects of it could be linked to guided missiles. It was decided that the appointment should be deferred.

William Skardon was kept up to date with these deliberations and was doing his best to secure Nunn May employment and also circumvent those who were placing obstacles in the way. He continued to argue that Nunn May would be a reliable and trustworthy employee. Again the question of what 'the Americans might think' was raised which Skardon pointedly sidelined. He thought the Americans should be told that he was working on non classified work for a private company.

The matter was discussed with officials from the Ministry of Supply. It was said that the Managing Director of Pye Radio, Mr C. Stanley, was an awkward Irishman, whose approach to the Ministry, was designed to embarrass them. It was recorded at the meeting that Nunn May was just the sort of person who would solve the problems faced by Pye Radio. It was also said that exchange of information with the U.S. Navy regarding guided missile systems would be halted if they were to learn that Nunn May was involved in this field. Dr Wansborough Jones, Principal Scientific Adviser to the Ministry said that telling the Americans that Nunn May was working in a private capacity was not acceptable. He was not being obstructive and could see the argument from both sides. Had the Ministry really explored all the possibilities relating to Nunn May's employment? The same ground was discussed yet again and Wansborough Jones then suggested that an approach be made to Dr Jacob Bronowski, Chief Scientific Adviser to the Coal Board.

What had seemed a promising opening at first was now in danger of being rejected for political reasons. The difficulties had now got to the stage whereby it was envisaged that a joint meeting between the Ministry of Labour, the Ministry of Supply and the Foreign Office should be arranged in order to find a way through these problems. There was a further meeting at the House of Commons between the Parliamentary Secretary for the Ministry of Supply, Brigadier Low, and representatives of the Home Office. The Minister of Supply, Mr Duncan Sandys, had told Low he should see Mr Stanley from Pye Radio. He should explain that it was their view, that the Americans would take a poor view of this form of employment. Stanley should be advised not to offer Nunn May a job. As regards other options, Duncan Sandys said he would speak to the Ministry of Fuel and Power regarding the Coal Board job. The Home Office reiterated their concerns at the delay in securing Nunn May employment despite their best efforts and those of the Ministry of Labour. The task had up to now taken seven months. It was pointed out that during this time the Foreign Office had been alarmed that Nunn May might have secured a job in Argentina. Brigadier Low said he understood these points of view but the potentially unfavourable American reaction had confirmed them. He would not raise the matter formally with the Foreign Office although if the Home Office were to sound them out, he would have no objection. If the Foreign Office view did not coincide with that of the Ministry of Supply they would consult officially.

During the period from February to July 1953, the issue of future employment was uppermost in Nunn May's mind but prison life and those he had encountered there refused to go away and also the press remained eager for another scoop.

On 12 April 1953, the *Empire News* printed a story about a Frenchman called Yves George Harrant. He had been a French Resistance leader during World War II, but had been found guilty of shooting a beautiful French model, Michel Lecomte, with intent to murder, outside the Berkeley Hotel in London. He had fired three shots, but she survived the ordeal. Harrant went to prison and served part of his sentence in Wakefield where he met Nunn May. He alleged that they had been friendly in prison and that he could provide documentation to enable

Nunn May to work anywhere in Europe. Nunn May had encountered him in prison where he had been the only person able to converse with him in French. Harrant was eventually released and deported to France. Nothing more was heard from him.

During July, Special Branch heard from Dublin, that Nunn May would be going to Prague, to work there for two years. The story was that a Patrick Malone, born in England in Felixstowe, on 11 May 1917 and holding a British passport, but now resident in Ballymore, Ireland, was applying for an Irish passport and would pass it on to Nunn May. MI5 alerted the passport offices in Britain and in Dublin. This turned out to be speculation but Malone was to surface again in October.

In May Nunn May went to stay, for ten days, with his aunts at Trevose, Holme Lane, Allithwaite, Grange over Sands and he also visited his sister Mary at 45 Pitmaston Court, Goodby Road, Moseley, Birmingham. In the middle of May 1953, he went to stay with Arthur Parker-Rhodes at 20 Sedley Taylor Road, Cambridge, where there was no telephone. This was also the address of a Raymond David de Longueuil. Parker-Rhodes was well known to MI5 as having strong Communist sympathies. It appears that Nunn May's departure from Chalfont St. Peter escaped the attention of those who were supposedly monitoring his movements but he was ultimately traced by the Cambridge Constabulary. He spent some time in Cambridge during June, whilst at the same time making himself available for job interviews.

On 23 June 1953, Mary, Alan's sister, telephoned Ralph at Chalfont St. Peter to say that Alan had asked her to keep some time free in early August and come to Cambridge. He had jokingly remarked that she might have to stay in a tent. The people at the Cambridge address seemed a bit strange and lived both in the house and a caravan and Mary was a bit puzzled by it. On 25 July, Ralph telephoned Mary, in Birmingham, from Chalfont St. Peter and she confirmed that she would be able to go to Cambridge.

What followed next must have sounded very odd to those intercepting the call. Mary then asked Ralph if he knew about 'it'. Ralph said yes, but he had to keep it very quiet, 'it' had not been going on for very long. They both thought it a good and excellent thing. Ralph had met 'her' and thought her nice. Mary would hear all about it tomorrow and meet 'her', but didn't think she could go to Cambridge the following weekend. Ralph then asked Mary if Alan had told her all about 'it' in his letter to which Mary replied, 'yes, that they were getting married'. Ralph then said, 'that it all had to be kept very dark.' Jackie (Ralph's wife) then spoke to Mary and told her that she must be discreet, but thought it was an excellent thing. Mary thought that all this telephoning was very rash.

Alan Nunn May had presumably asked his sister and brother to be very discreet and warned them about using the telephone. He may well have realised that all calls were being monitored and remained anxious about intrusion from the press. His address at Cambridge did not have a telephone but on 23 July a warrant was applied for to intercept all mail arriving at and leaving the address in Sedley Taylor Road.

CHAPTER NINETEEN

On 1 August 1953, Alan Nunn May was married by special licence to Hildegarde Pauline Ruth Broda at Cambridge Registry Office. The witnesses were Peter Arundel Jewel, and Ralph Nunn May. Afterwards they drove back in Parker-Rhodes's car to Hildegarde's address at Chesterton Hall, Cambridge. There was a small gathering present to celebrate the event. Among those present were Paul Broda her twelve year old son from her first marriage; Gerda Newmark, who lived at Buckland Common in Buckinghamshire ; Alan and Christine Ness, Architects who lived in Wigmore Street, London and one or two neighbours from nearby. After a short time the couple left for a honeymoon.

This seems to have caught MI5 by surprise, who only got to know about it through newspaper reports in the *Sunday Dispatch* and *Sunday Express*. There had been no previous hint of any relationship with Hildegarde Broda. What must have exercised their minds even more was that Hildegarde's first husband was Engelbert Broda. The Brodas had come to the United Kingdom as refugees in 1938. He had been interned at the beginning of the war as had been reported to be the leader of the London Group of the Austrian Communist Party. He had worked alongside Alan Nunn May at the Cavendish Laboratory during the war and had been engaged on the Tube Alloys Project. The security services were well aware of Engelbert Broda's communist attachments but this concern was set to one side because of his contribution to the Tube Alloys Project. It was also known that after his divorce in

September 1946, Engelbert, had returned to Austria sometime in 1947. At the time of his return, the Americans were informed because of suspicions that he might be taking with him vital information, but this had not been followed up.

The question of who had recruited Alan Nunn May at Cambridge during the thirties remained an unresolved issue for MI5. Nunn May had refused to reveal who it was. He had commented to Skardon that the person was 'well out of reach'. Could it have been Engelbert Broda? He had worked alongside Alan Nunn May at the Cavendish Laboratory. When Nunn May returned from Canada in September 1945 he was under surveillance. It was known that he visited Cambridge on 16–17 October 1945 where amongst others he met Engelbert Broda. He also had lunch with Broda and Lew Kowarski on 14 January 1946. MI5 still had no proof but they began to convince themselves that this was a strong possibility. Engelbert Broda was now resident in Austria.

Alan Nunn May and his wife Hildegarde settled into married life at her home in a ground floor flat at Chesterton Hall, Cambridge.

Hildegarde Pauline Ruth Broda was the daughter of Ludwig and Elsie Gerwing. She was born on 12 March 1911 in Aachen, Germany. She obtained a medical degree in Vienna and obtained Austrian citizenship after her marriage to Engelbert Broda on 11 September 1936. On 23 May 1938, they arrived in the UK as refugees from Nazi oppression. At the outbreak of war they were classed as aliens, but Hildegarde was exempted from internment in November 1939 by virtue of her medical degree which meant she could fulfil an important function at that time. Engelbert on the other hand had to appeal against internment. His appeal was supported by Sir Lawrence Bragg as he was considered to be a valued scientist who could support the work of the Cavendish Laboratory. He was released from internment in December 1939. A child Paul Martin Andrew was born in London on 15 March 1939.

From 1940, Hildegarde, lived in and around London. She and her husband were often separated because of their jobs. In October 1942 she obtained a job in an Austrian day nursery for children in Fitzroy Avenue, London NW3 where she was able to live on the premises. From July 1943 until August 1944 she became part time Assistant Medical

Officer of Health to a children's home at Hanworth, Middlesex. She was then living at Lambode Road, London NW3. From there she went to work at Culdulnel Hospital, Inverness, until March 1945, when she went to Cambridge to join her husband and became Assistant Medical Officer of Health for schools. She remained there until her second marriage in 1953, apart from staying in London between October 1947 and March 1948. Between May 1938 and March 1945 she had resided at eighteen different addresses. They included three other hospitals; Queen's Hospital, Hackney, Stoke Mandeville Hospital and North Middlesex County Hospital in Edmonton, London. During this time she was taking care of her young son and they were separated from their father who was working in Cambridge. She managed occasional weekend visits to London, and was a supporter of the Paddington Branch of the Austrian Centre, where her husband was a leading member.

The constant changes of address must have placed a great deal of strain on their marriage. She and Engelbert separated and were divorced on 24 September 1946 although they seemed to remain on good terms with one another afterwards.

Hildegarde seemed to have a great empathy with children and she loved her career as a doctor. She also had interests outside medicine. She was secretary to the Cambridge Peace Council, secretary to the local branch of the International Womens' Day Committee, and a member of the Britain-China Friendship Association.

She acquired a great many friends and kept up regular communication with many of them. On her marriage to Alan Nunn May, she was always happy for people to stay at their home and seemed to have been the driving force and more outgoing than Alan. She seems to have been very friendly with Eric Hobsbawn, a prominent historian and lecturer at Birkbeck College, University of London at the time. He held strong Marxist beliefs which attracted wide scale criticism. She also knew John Desmond Bernal, a pioneer in the field of X-ray crystallography, who had worked at Cambridge in the thirties. He was very prominent in political life and was a great supporter of the Soviet Union. Hildegarde was very keen that they should all meet up.

MI5 kept a phone tap at the Chesterton Hall address and maintained an interest in their contacts. It appeared that nearly all of them had Communist or Marxist leanings of some kind and the security services held files on them.

In December 1953, there was to be a farewell dinner in honour of Lawrence Bragg from the Cavendish Laboratory which Alan was diffident about attending, for fear of causing embarrassment to some of those present. He and his wife, however, did attend a gathering of friends at 19A St. John's Avenue, Leatherhead in Surrey which was the home of Dr James Nelson and his wife Doris, over the weekend of 2 and 3 January. The Chief Constable of Surrey was asked to monitor the event and his staff were able to identify those present from their car registration numbers. This would indicate that the guests including the Nunn Mays' were prosperous. Those present were all members of the Communist Party. One person who stood out amongst those that were identified, was Norman Veal. He was working as a Research Assistant for the Medical Research Council, at Hammersmith Hospital. It was Veal who had approached Nunn May in the Montreal Laboratory in 1945 to discuss whether they should pass on secrets to the Russians. Nunn May had been advised by his Russian operator to have nothing to do with Veal. Veal was also mentioned in the Canadian Royal Commission Report into the whole affair. The two presumably had much gossip to catch up on.

Hildegarde seems to have been resolute in her actions and was giving Alan moral support. But she also had to face up to a challenge from a local councillor in Cambridge who wanted her removed from her job.

In November 1953, Captain A.C. Taylor, a member of Cambridge City Council and proprietor of the *Cambridge Daily News* questioned the City Council concerning the continuing employment of Dr Broda. He said that he had been approached by ratepayers and ex-servicemen who protested at her continuing employment as she was married to a man who had sold secrets to another country. The City Council was about to increase her salary. He was ruled out of order and left the meeting. After the meeting, Alderman Rackham was quoted as saying, 'Dr Broda is a good medical officer and so long as she does her work well, who she marries has nothing to do with anyone. Whatever the man did, he paid the penalty and it is wrong to persecute his wife.'

Captain Taylor was not to be deflected and tabled a motion in January 1954 to the County Council for Hildegarde Broda's employment to be terminated. By the time this meeting was held, the issue had gathered a significant amount of publicity and was reported in the local and national press. The Nunn May's sought legal advice from Sidney Silverman a solicitor from London, and on his advice, they engaged a shorthand writer to attend the meeting.

The council meeting provoked caustic comments from some of its members and resentments came to the surface. Not only was Hildegarde under scrutiny but the spotlight was focused yet again on her husband Alan. The following are extracts from the report of the proceedings by the *Cambridge Daily News*.

Captain Taylor had started by saying that in approaching the City Council first, this was an opportunity for Dr Broda to tender her resignation to those who employed her. Last year without considering her employment she married Dr Nunn May. There was an interruption by Alderman Stubbs, 'What's wrong with that?'

Captain Taylor went on, 'Dr Nunn May was a very fine research worker in a laboratory in Cambridge'. Councillor Mole interrupted to ask if Captain Taylor was going to bring Dr Nunn May's children into the debate as well.

Captain Taylor continued, 'the lady came here with a history of communist involvement, and her husband sold this country to the communists. He has been employed by someone I strongly suspect of being a strong communist in this city. It is not fair to the lady that she should be put in a position where she may be suspected of indoctrinating the children with whom she comes into contact.' A council member called out, 'Rubbish'. Captain Taylor said he had been approached by ratepayers, ex Servicemen and associations to protest and ask that the services of Dr Broda be terminated. 'How do you think the mothers of a good many thousand British soldiers feel towards anyone who has been traitor to his own country? He was in possession of vital atomic secrets. He gave these secrets to a foreign country and they may or may not have cost thousands of lives.'

Alderman Stubbs pointed out that the Council should be dealing with Dr Broda, not with her husband.

Captain Taylor went on, 'This is a free country and Dr Broda can marry who she likes, (cries of hear, hear). I have liberty to say in notice of this kind what the public have asked me to say. It is this: we don't like the way you have shown your appreciation of what this country has done for you, and you should leave public service.'

Councillor Hearn seconded the motion. He said, 'it was quite wrong to pay rates to support the greatest traitor since Judas Iscariot'.

Councillor Ockleston commented, 'If Dr Broda were to be handling adults, he would not support the motion, but she was coming into contact with children and was in a position to turn them to Communism. There was no reason why she could not be transferred to some other job.'

Councillor Newman said, 'I don't know if Dr Broda is a Communist. I don't care two damns if she is and I am more qualified to speak on this that any of the other speakers. Three of my own children attend schools in this county or city and they come under the attention of Dr Broda. What attention they have had has been good. If she indoctrinates my children she will only have the opportunity of doing it five minutes in perhaps six months. I can take care of any five minutes she has with my children in ten minutes I have after.'

Councillor Mole described the motion as, 'A dirty, filthy attack. Was there any evidence that she had indoctrinated children or had not carried out her duties towards them? Judging by the people who have been to see me to protest against this crime, parents think she has carried out her job second to none, and is one of the finest medical officers we have ever had in this city. Her whole life is wrapped up in children and their welfare. Was it Captain Taylor's business to go into private lives or introduce the filthy system of McCarthyism? Dr Nunn May had served a prison sentence for a crime he had committed, how many more sentences was he going to serve. Was Captain Taylor going to attack his children and say what schools they should go to? Captain Taylor had committed the crime of being a traitor to democracy. Turn this wicked filthy resolution into a vote of confidence for Dr Broda.'

Councillor Shelley said, 'Dr Broda's work was carried out in a really wonderful manner for the benefit of the children.'

Alderman Edwards said that, 'if he had been told that Captain Taylor, for whom he had the greatest respect, was going to move the resolution of this character he would have hotly disputed it. He held no brief whatever for Mr May who was charged, found guilty and sentenced for a crime he, personally, abhorred. But was it right that having the sword of justice brought down upon him and having discharged his sentence, they should now put over the head of a woman who in love had married him, a sword of vengeance? There was nothing so cruel, nothing so wicked. It would mean a life sentence for this woman and send her into a wilderness of poverty and humiliation from which she could never recover. The idea was un-British.'

He continued, 'Before you place a vote against this honourable woman whose only crime is that she married a traitor, let me say I hope and believe that her influence on May will be to make him a better citizen, and that she will carry on to do grand and noble work in Cambridge as a medical officer.'

Alderman Mrs Rackham pointed out that, 'The Council's joint committee could not concern itself with the dismissal of any officer. The power rested entirely with the City Council who engaged Dr Broda and the Council could only recommend a dismissal to that authority. When the marriage had taken place last August, it had been fully reported in the local press and there had not been a single protest from any parents of the thousands of children dealt with by Dr Broda'. She went on to say that she had a sheaf of letters from individuals and also from the headmistress of the local school for delicate children where important work for spastics was carried on. All of the letters spoke highly of Dr Broda.

Captain Taylor responded to the debate by saying that he had made it clear that he did not think of Dr Broda as anything other than as a highly intelligent woman doing a hard job of work. He continued, 'But we in this country always wait until the horse has gone from the stable and then we lock the door. If there is any possible chance of any danger, any question of young children under her charge being used in the wrong way, then we ought to find employment for her in a less dangerous job. Knowing the associations there, I don't think we should run the risk of employing the lady in a job which she might use as a rod for our own back ... or perhaps this country will wake up too late when a Communist Government takes over.'

Captain Taylor's motion to terminate Dr Broda's contract was rejected without calling for a show of hands. Hildegarde was to receive a great deal of support from her working colleagues and friends throughout the ordeal. She could now carry on with the work that she loved.

As regards Alan Nunn May and his job prospects there seemed to be no progress. He was doing a small amount of work for Dr Wooster of Crystal Structures in Cambridge but this was not significant. He went to see the Ministry of Labour pointing out that nine months had elapsed with no progress. The Ministry of Supply seemed less than interested in his situation despite anxieties raised by the Home Office. The following letter illustrates the difficulties.

Ministry of Labour and National Service
Almack House
King Street
London S.W.1

Dr A.N. May
Chesterton Hall
Chesterton Road
Cambridge

31st October 1953

Dear Dr May,

I have your letter of 27th October.

With regard to your suggestion that you might have a talk with someone from the Ministry of Supply, I do not think this would advance matters at all. In view of what happened over the Pye project, we think it would be unprofitable to pursue any further projects with that Ministry.

There are however other fields of work in which the Ministry of Supply would not be interested, and it is there that your and our efforts should now be directed.

As regards the question of you yourself exploring the possibility of getting financial assistance, we assume that what you have in mind relates to work for which funds might perhaps be made available from some non Governmental source. We should be very interested to hear what progress you can make in this direction.

Meantime, we are not in any way relaxing our efforts to assist you, and I will at once let you know if anything promising results.

Yours sincerely

N.R. Cantelo

Nunn May even suggested to the Ministry that it might be better if he sought a job overseas. He had already discussed this with a friend who said that they would welcome his expertise in India.

On 18 December 1953 there was a Cabinet Meeting with Winston Churchill, the Prime Minister, in the Chair. Among those present were Anthony Eden, Foreign Secretary; David Maxwell Fyfe, Home Secretary; and Harold A. Watkinson, Minister of Labour. They were reminded that they had received reassurances, that Nunn May would not leave the country immediately on his release from prison. They were also told that despite the efforts of the Ministry of Labour, he had been unable to secure employment. His funds were running low and this might persuade him to accept employment overseas. Again they felt this would give rise to adverse public comment, not least in the United States. They urged the Minister of Labour to try harder.

Watkinson went on to say that these efforts would not succeed unless supported by public funds. It might be possible for the Department of Scientific and Industrial Research (DSIR) to subsidise an employer willing to engage him on a grant of between £500 to £2,000 per annum. Maxwell Fyfe was not keen on the idea but nevertheless thought this might be the best way of dissuading Nunn May from working abroad.

The Lord President of the Council, the Marquess of Salisbury, disagreed. He did not see why a traitor to the country should be provided with employment under the auspices and subsidy of a government department. Nunn May's knowledge of atomic matters was out of date, and he was of no value to a potential enemy. If he went abroad the situation could be explained to the public.

It was then explained to the Cabinet that there was a crystallographer in Cambridge who would employ Nunn May. He was already doing work for the DSIR and if there was a promise of further work no direct payment from public funds would be necessary. This was deemed unsatisfactory by the Cabinet since it involved the Government in negotiations with a third party. Also, that person was a communist, and as such was thought to be unreliable.

In conclusion, the Cabinet decided that it was not in the public interest for Nunn May to seek employment abroad and therefore they should seek to provide money from secret funds in order that he should be employed in this country for at least twelve months. Maxwell Fyfe promised to make the arrangements.

As regards any security issues MI5 became preoccupied again with the activities of a Patrick Richard Malone. In July they had been warned by intelligence from Dublin that Malone was to acquire a passport for Nunn May and secure him work in Czechloslovakia. The rumour was not substantiated but Malone was now back in the U.K. and was lodging in Eccles, Lancashire. He had obtained employment locally and appeared to be settling there for a while. This caused MI5 to ensure that his movements and associates were monitored closely. They regarded Malone as a shady character who was not earning much money. But investigations in Dublin had revealed that he had inherited monies from the sale of land in Ireland, but seemed to be erratic in his behaviour, and spent money wastefully. A great deal of time was spent by the security services in the UK and in Dublin investigating him but eventually he returned there without making any approaches to Nunn May. Malone's activities raised yet again the concerns as to Nunn May's leaving the country. All ports were informed to be aware if anyone answering Nunn May's description tried to leave. They could not prevent him from doing so but might be able to dissuade him from such a course of action.

The Nunn May's marriage had not escaped the attention of the United States. They were aware of the link with Hildegarde's first husband, Engelbert, and the security issues surrounding him. They wanted to know what information the British had on Hildegarde and whether she had been involved in espionage.

CHAPTER TWENTY

The following year, in January 1954, Nunn May at last secured paid employment with Crystal Structures Ltd. of Cambridge, a company which was only indirectly associated with the University. It was run by Dr W.A. Wooster, his wife, Nora Wooster and their son Paul. Nunn May was engaged to perform crystallographic research in their laboratories. It was not classified work and he must have been delighted to secure employment so near to his home. It had been a tortuous route and he would not have been aware of the work which had been undertaken by the various ministries as well as pressure applied by MI5 to secure the job. It was agreed that his employment would be subsidised to the sum of £2,000 over two years. There appeared to be some argument as to whose Whitehall budget would provide the money and how long it would go on for, but the sum of £120 per month was paid over to the University of Cambridge and then forwarded to Crystal Structures to conceal the source of the money. After twelve months the situation was to be reviewed when hopefully, it might be possible to reduce the sums of money involved. At least now, Nunn May could properly settle down and it was a problem solved for the Home Office and MI5.

Crystal Structures Ltd., were based in a two storey extension to Dr Wooster's residence at 339 Cherry Hinton Road, Cambridge. The laboratory was called the Brooklyn Crystallographic Laboratory and there was a ground floor workshop, equipped with a lathe, drilling and milling machines. The laboratory was engaged in consultative and development work for Crystal Structures who specialised in apparatus designed for crystallographic work. The company's main interest was the structural and physical properties of materials, they were also doing work for Technicolour and the Post Office.

Nunn May was to compile a report of his work there for the period from January 1954 to June 1955. In it he described how he decided to work mainly on the properties of semi-conductors. He knew this was becoming of increasing importance in fields of electrical engineering to produce direct current for electroplating processes and, perhaps even more importantly, to be incorporated in transistors which were by then, rapidly replacing radio valves. He proposed to investigate the relationship of their physical structure and electrical properties by the means of X-rays. (Semiconductors would ultimately become a major component of computers).

He describes in his report how a high vacuum apparatus was purchased for the work. This necessitated adapting the plans for rebuilding the laboratory for which the Woosters' had already requested planning permission. Eventually this was granted and the work completed. While waiting for this work to be finished Nunn May took responsibility for the development of the electronic servo mechanism in a micro densitometer which Dr Wooster had designed. This instrument could measure the intensity of blackening of X-ray films.

The arrangements had suited Nunn May very well although he had occasion to disagree with Wooster regarding the testing of an instrument before delivery to a customer. Nunn May wanted more time for testing while Wooster had promised a delivery date which , he felt, ought to be met. This coincided with a period when Nunn May's adopted son, John Michael, was coming home from hospital and he did not feel he was in a position to work overtime to meet the deadline.

In his report, Nunn May also refers to the fact that his work was only possible by virtue of an anonymous gift and that ultimately, through his researches he would become self supporting by the time the money ran out. In his last paragraph he says, 'May I in conclusion express my sincere gratitude to the donor for the generosity of his gift, and my appreciation of the unique opportunity it has given me. I can only hope that I shall be able to justify his action by my scientific work.' Such remarks would suggest that Nunn May was unaware of the source of his grant or perhaps he was choosing his words with care.

During this period, Hildegarde Nunn May was earning £1300 per annum and the two salaries combined represented a very comfortable living. It was enough for them both to contemplate a holiday in Austria during Easter 1954, Hildegarde was a naturalised Austrian. Another problem was therefore to confront the Home Office and MI5. What would they do when Alan Nunn May applied for a passport?

The Foreign Office response was, '...it would be most unwise to endanger the improvement in our relations to the United States in atomic energy matters brought about by the Bermuda Conference, by risking the departure of Nunn May behind the Iron Curtain and thus raising once again adverse reaction in the United States set up by the cases of Fuchs, Pontecorvo and Maclean. There is no reason why we should facilitate the departure of Nunn May, by giving him a passport for the ostensible purpose of a holiday in Austria, since it would not be difficult for him, once in that country, to slip behind the Iron Curtain. In these circumstances it should be quite possible to meet any Parliamentary criticism about the refusal of passport facilities to Nunn May, since as you know, the Foreign Secretary has discretion to refuse a passport in those rare cases where the activities of an individual are notoriously unreliable or dangerous...' Nunn May was no doubt relishing his life as a free man, but not sufficiently free to enjoy a holiday of his choice.

The possibility of foreign travel was soon to resurface. In July, Crystal Structures Ltd., were planning to display some of their instruments at an exhibition in connection with an international conference on crystallography in Paris. They wanted Nunn May to accompany the directors of the firm and assist in the demonstration of their equipment. As a preliminary to the application for a passport, Dr Nora Wooster, one of the directors, sought help from the Vice Chancellor of Cambridge University.

The Foreign Office were pressed in the light of circumstances to decide once more on the issue of a passport. They were briefed by Graham Mitchell, Deputy Director General of MI5. He referred back to the Cabinet's deliberations in December 1953. They wanted Nunn May to remain in the U.K. and their decision to provide financial support towards employment would give some assurance that this would happen. The real issue was that they did not want Nunn May to become a permanent domicile behind the Iron Curtain. If they refused a visit to Paris on business, or for that matter a holiday, this might be seen as petty minded by Nunn May and that there was no future remaining in the U.K. After all if he was really determined to leave it would be very difficult to stop him. Mitchell agreed that if Nunn May disappeared behind the Iron Curtain relations with the USA would be strained on atomic energy matters. Although he would be unable to provide the Russians with useful information and would be just one more trained atomic scientist, Nunn May might well believe that the Russians would readily recognise his reputation and offer him a job of some importance.

Mitchell said that there was a risk that being in France would make it easier for him to be spirited behind the Iron Curtain. It had been suggested that Nunn May be issued with a passport valid only for France but this was most unusual if not unprecedented. On balance, Mitchell was of the view that, given Nunn May's current situation, it would be in his best interests to remain in the U.K. and not abscond. He had sufficient confidence that he would not disappear for him to be granted a full passport. If this judgement proved to be misplaced there would be some damage to Anglo U.S. relations but no threat to security.

The Foreign Office did not agree. It was still too early to take the risk of letting Nunn May go abroad with the blessing of Her Majesty's Government.

MI5 decided that given this decision and their misgivings they would talk to Nunn May in advance of any official rejection of his request for a passport to go to Paris. It was decided that Jim Skardon should get the job of seeing Nunn May since he had got to know him reasonably well. His report on their meeting was as follows:

On 4 June 1954 I saw Alan Nunn May at Chesterton Hall, Chesterton Road, Cambridge. At this address with his wife Dr Broda he occupies a ground floor flat.

He received me in a fairly cordial manner.

I told him that I had been instructed quite officially to see him and to inform him of the result of consideration given to an enquiry made on his behalf as to the possibility of the grant of a British Passport to him. He said straight away that he had applied for one last year when he wanted to take a skiing holiday in Austria with his wife. It had been refused. Crystal Products for whom he works want to display certain technical implements at an exhibition in Paris in July in connection with a conference on crystallography, and Dr Nora Wooster, a director, did say, she would make enquiries to see if May could get a passport for the purpose of attending the equipment as a demonstrator. He did not know which channel she was using to make this enquiry.

I informed May that

> He would not be granted a passport during this summer.
> This was not a permanent disqualification but merely a decision to deal with the present enquiry.
> It was thought that the grant of a passport for the purpose, with resulting visit to Paris would certainly evoke Press notices and these would be embarrassing to him and to H.M. Government.
> The authorities had noted with pleasure the fact that he was settled in a job and domestically. The Security Authorities claimed some share in producing this happy situation.

I added as my opinion, which he was at liberty to quote only as such, the belief that the political climate in Anglo American relations did not encourage the Foreign Secretary to take a risk in this case. Negotiations for the exchange of secret information were at a critical stage and any adverse publicity engendered as a result of the free movement of May on the continent could not be encouraged.

May understood the situation exactly. He hoped that a later application would be more successful and when I offered to advise in

due time, he said he thought he would be able to judge when the time was ripe for himself.
He does not want us to reply to the enquiry raised. He will be able to deal with this himself.
He was surprisingly reasonable
W.J. Skardon

We do not know what Nunn May made of this meeting but given Skardon's report he seems to have accepted the decision with equanimity. Skardon seems to have trodden very carefully and diplomatically through their meeting and it was perhaps fortunate that they had established a rapport on previous occasions.

Despite these rebuffs Nunn May's wife, Hildegarde applied for Citizenship of the United Kingdom in August 1954.

In September 1954, Jim Skardon was contacted by Ralph Nunn May, saying he wished to discuss with him certain urgent matters which had cropped up. As far as Skardon knew there was nothing untoward as regards his brother Alan's situation. He agreed to meet Ralph at the Savile Club, Brook Street, London on 10 September.

Skardon was anxious to know at the outset if there was a problem relating to Alan of which he was not aware. Ralph said straightaway that he wanted to raise matters personal to himself which related to his own business affairs. He said that Skardon must know that he used to work for the Ministry of Information and subsequently with the Crown Film Unit and be aware of his current job situation. Skardon responded that they knew nothing more about him than had been pertinent to the enquiries that had been necessary at the time of his brother's arrest. Skardon was of course aware of Ralph's degree of support before the trial and during Alan's time in prison and afterwards.

Ralph then explained his situation more fully. He was a director of Anvil Films Ltd, whose other staff included Ken Cameron, Richard Warren, and Ken Scrivener. They had achieved some success in gaining contracts of various kinds for an American organisation based in Paris. Another large substantial contract was in the offing, all arrangements had been made, when it was cancelled without warning. He spoke to his contact in Paris who was negotiating the contract and had been told that a Joe Evans, Information Officer at the United States Embassy in London had for security reasons vetoed the contract because of Ralph's relationship with his brother. Ralph had spoken to Joe Evans about this and was told that the cancellation was not for any security reasons but Anvil Films Ltd. had too large a share in the contracts being awarded. Ralph was not satisfied with the story. The American associates in Paris were angry and had decided not to award any of the contracts. Some discussions followed during which it was remarked that there was a greater likelihood of his organisation gaining contracts if Ralph Nunn May was not on the Board of Directors. The result of this was that Ken Cameron and Richard Warren had formed another company trading as World Mirror Productions Ltd.

There were other issues of seeking work which were troubling him. He had written to Major E.G. Fraser, Directorate of Military Training, War Office, Chessington, Surrey. He had received no reply.

He was in discussions with a Naval Officer on the Admiralty Training side who thought that his company could produce training films for them. Nothing happened.

Was there anything that he could do to put right any doubts about his loyalty that the security services might harbour, simply because he was Alan Nunn May's brother? Skardon responded by saying that the MI5 records about him stopped at the conclusion of the enquiries into his brother's conduct at the time of Alan's arrest. This, however, was not true. They had monitored Ralph's visits to his brother in prison and recorded all telephone calls and mail to Ralph's house when Alan was released from prison. He did say that his department had not made any enquiry about his character which was true although they knew that he had been a President of the National Union of Students. He told Ralph that he thought he was being over sensitive regarding his contacts with British authorities. As regards the American situation he could do very little to help. He would make enquiries and if his suspicions were unfounded he would tell him so. On the other hand if there was some substance to them he, Skardon, would have to be very careful as to what he revealed. Ralph appeared to understand Skardon's comments but he must have felt that the stain of Alan's misdemeanours had spread to him and his livelihood was being adversely affected.

As the lunch progressed Ralph began to talk more about his brother. He said that neither he nor the rest of his family were convinced that Alan was a member of the Communist Party. When Alan left for Canada in 1943, he had dined with Ralph and his wife the evening before his departure. They had met up at his Mother's funeral in 1946, but he was stupefied when he heard the news on the radio that Alan had been arrested. When the announcement gave information about Canadian espionage he was sure his brother's name would be mentioned. On hearing the news he had telephoned Bow Street Police Station but had not been encouraged to go there that evening. He saw Alan immediately after his first appearance before the Magistrate. He tried to obtain some claim of innocence from him but all he said was that he was there because of the statement he had made. From that time onwards he was sure of Alan's guilt. Skardon commented that Alan had never been forthcoming about the events which led to his treachery and he was not surprised by this. Alan was a man of considerable tenacity and the odd man out in the family.

Ralph said that when Alan came to stay with him and his wife after his release from Wakefield Prison, he had become an awful nuisance around the house. They were deeply grateful when Hildegarde Broda took him off their hands. The latest news he had of his brother was that he and Hildegarde had adopted a month old boy. (Hildegarde already had a son, from her first marriage to Engelbert Broda, Paul Martin Andrew, born 15 March 1939, who was living with her). Ralph thought his brother slightly mad to do this. He had been a witness at the marriage ceremony but concluded by saying that there was now little contact between him and his brother. There was an elder brother Edward but he appeared to have distanced himself from Alan.

Ralph had done his best to support his brother while in prison. He had organised the delivery of books and periodicals to him and visited periodically. He had also protested vehemently when Alan was moved from the Open Prison at Leyhill, back to the confines of Wakefield Prison, apparently without reason. He and his wife supported him during his imprisonment and after he was released. But this had been a strain on them as they clearly had little in common with Alan apart from family loyalty. He must also have thought that this disaster in the family was still interfering with his ability to continue a normal life.

After this meeting, Skardon, examined MI5 files for traces of any recent vetting of Ralph Nunn May or the two companies Anvil Films Ltd and World Mirror Productions Ltd. He found nothing. He was to report to Ralph, that his fears of the Security Services interfering with his livelihood were baseless. There was no feedback concerning the American problem.

The information gleaned by MI5 from the telephone and letter checks on the Nunn May's address began to diminish and the decision was reached that monitoring by MI5 should be withdrawn. They wished to retain the fall back position provided for them by the Cambridgeshire Constabulary who continued to monitor activities and keep them informed. At one point the possibility was raised of recruiting the Nunn May's 'daily woman' as an informant. This was discounted as disclosure might lead to alienation and feelings of insecurity.

CHAPTER TWENTY-ONE

In May 1955, Hildegarde Nunn May, requested that she be granted a passport in order to go on holiday to Austria with her children. The Foreign Office's response was to refuse her application. This was to precipitate yet another series of correspondence between the Foreign Office and MI5 who put forward the arguments for and against such a decision.

The Foreign Office telephoned MI5 on 10 May saying that they were disposed to refuse Hildegarde Nunn May a passport on the same grounds as those applied to her husband. Graham Mitchell, Head of D Branch, (Counterespionage) at MI5 responded by saying that the refusal of Alan Nunn May's passport by the Foreign Office was entirely on political not security grounds. If the Foreign Office proposed to use the same grounds for refusal MI5 would have nothing to say on the matter. He doubted whether there were good security reasons for denying her a passport.

On 25 May, Street of the Foreign Office telephoned Mitchell again. He asked Mitchell whether he might ask one of MI5's officers to see Alan Nunn May and explain to him the difficulties that his wife's passport request posed to the authorities. They could suggest that if his wife applied again in say three months time, she might have better luck.

Mitchell asked, how would they respond, if Nunn May were to ask if he would get a passport in three months time as well? He was less than keen on the idea. He telephoned A.J. de la Mare at the Foreign Office saying that they did not feel they could comply with the suggestion. Mitchell's officers could not discuss the politics of the issue with them as it would undermine their relationship with the Nunn Mays'. If the Foreign Office were thinking of reconsidering their decision, why not write to Hildegard Nunn May directly or possibly invite her to the Foreign Office for an interview? De la Mare concurred with these views.

He wrote back to Mitchell on 8 June saying that he agreed there was no case on security grounds for refusing Hildegarde Nunn May a passport. But, De la Mare responded with the following comments:

> There is always the risk that she might be intending to defect and, as a first step, to reclaim the Austrian nationality which she possessed before her marriage. In that case her husband would have strong compassionate grounds for being allowed to join her.
> If the Nunn Mays' were to defect there would be an outcry in the press here and in America, and this would prejudice Anglo American relations generally and the atomic energy agreements in particular. The responsible departments here therefore propose to recommend to the Secretary of State that he should withhold a passport from Mrs Nunn May for the present and that she should be told that her case will be reviewed if she applies again later on.
> If however this decision had to be defended in Parliament, we could not give the real reason for it and could only say that it had been taken on security grounds.

The passage of time and with it Alan Nunn May's increasingly out of date knowledge of atomic physics meant it was no longer a security risk. Political expediency and the relationship with the United States was of paramount importance. This threw back on to MI5's shoulders the need for their support on the 'security' aspect, despite the fact that they did not agree with it.

MI5 were to agree that if the decision had to be defended in Parliament they would concur with the security reasons and draft a reply in the event of a Parliamentary question.

On Monday 25 July 1955, Hildegarde Nunn May attended for

interview at the Passport Office with a Mr Rex. In the interview room prior to her arrival, Rex conferred with R.T. Reed from MI5 who was to act only as an observer and take notes. Rex said to Reed that he was very uneasy about the interview. He felt he had no right to ask some of the questions which the Foreign Office had suggested.

At noon they received a message to say that Hildegarde and Alan Nunn May were waiting outside. A message was relayed back that Mr Rex only wished to see Mrs Nunn May. A moment or two later the messenger returned saying that Mrs Nunn May had insisted on being accompanied by her husband. The message went back saying that Rex would only see Mrs Nunn May and not accompanied by her husband. Hildegarde Nunn May came to the interview room alone.

After a very diffident and tense start, Hildegarde talked about how she was a German subject who had acquired Austrian nationality through marriage to Engelbert Broda. She had been informed that after her marriage to Alan Nunn May she did not automatically qualify for British citizenship and had applied in 1955. The reason she wanted a passport was to go on holiday with her son Paul, from her first marriage, born 15 March 1939. Paul had been granted a British Passport in 1948 which had been renewed in 1953. This passport had been granted on a Court Order giving permission for Mrs Broda to take the child out of the country to see his father in Austria.

At this point Hildegarde's demeanour seemed to relax somewhat. She said that she intended to travel with her son to Austria but was unable to go with him since she did not have a passport. She wanted to go to Austria in October and see him. Asked why she had not asked about the progress of the passport application which she had submitted in May, she replied that she had been told that it was 'under consideration'.

Rex had no more questions and thanked Hildegarde for coming. She immediately asked for a decision about her passport and was told that it would be decided by a higher authority. On reaching the door she said, 'And what about my husband's passport?' Rex responded by saying that he was not empowered to discuss it.

She then asked Rex if a passport would now be granted to her husband. He said that he understood that this had been refused although he was in a position to re-apply.

Hildegarde said she could not understand why her husband had been refused a passport again, because when he came out of prison he had been interviewed by Mr Skardon of MI5 and told that while he could not be granted a passport at the moment he was invited to apply later on when there was a good chance that his application would be granted. Upon applying again, a passport had been refused. She said, 'It is extremely awkward you see. He needs his passport for his work and to visit international conferences'.

Rex replied that while that might be so, he understood that in his original application Nunn May had said he wanted his passport for a holiday. Rex now found himself in an awkward position and again said he was sorry but could not discuss her husband's case.

The interview was brought to a close.

The next day the Foreign Office telephoned Reed at MI5 and asked if he was preparing a note for them about the interview. Reed said he had been present as an observer. He was preparing a note for his MI5 director, but it was Rex's responsibility to send a report to the Foreign Office.

The following morning the Foreign Office telephoned Reed again. They had read Rex's account which he had ended by saying that he thought Mrs Nunn May had an ulterior motive in applying for a passport. Reed of MI5 did not agree with that assessment. Would he prepare an urgent note giving his version of the interview together with confirmation that neither Mr nor Mrs Nunn May possessed information of value. Reed said that neither of the Nunn May's possessed information of value nor were they employed on secret work.

Graham Mitchell, Head of D Branch, MI5, telephoned de la Mare at the Foreign Office. He confirmed Reed's view that he did not think that Hildegarde Nunn May had an ulterior motive in applying for a passport. Perhaps de la Mare should invite Rex and Reed round to the Foreign Office to reach an agreed opinion about what took place.

Mitchell went on to say that if the Cabinet were reconsidering the case of the Nunn Mays, they should not be provided with new damaging allegations without very good reason.

As he understood it, the reasons for not granting passports was, that if they were misused, atomic energy exchanges with the United States would be prejudiced. Since agreement had been reached on these exchanges, much of the validity of those reasons had disappeared.

De la Mare eventually agreed to amend Rex's report to the effect that nothing had occurred in the interview with Hildegarde to support claims of an ulterior motive.

Mitchell confirmed the view of MI5, in writing, to de la Mare. In his letter he also reminded the Foreign Office of the need to support Alan Nunn May's employment in the UK. They had not forgotten the wrangling that these arrangements had necessitated and which had taken up so much of everybody's time. He went on to emphasise that this issue was about to come up yet again:

'When the subsidy to Nunn May ends, probably in November next year, 1955, it is believed that he will seek a livelihood by approaching industrial firms with the fruits of his researches over the last two years. If he fails to find support form British firms he might seek it overseas. We cannot think however that this constitutes sufficient reason to continue to withhold a passport either from Nunn May or from his wife'.

A few days after her interview on 25 July 1955, Hildegarde Nunn May was granted a passport. But no passport had at that time been granted to Alan Nunn May.

Whilst working in Cambridge Nunn May asked Professor Mott at the Cavendish Laboratory in the University if he might attend lectures there. There was a flurry of communication which ended back at MI5. Mott did not want any bad publicity and he knew nothing of the two year benefaction, but he was told that he must accede to the request.

Six months later, it came to the attention of the Government that the East German Government might offer employment to Nunn May. Kathe Dornberger, a scientist from East Germany had visited the U.K. in connection with a conference organised by the Institute of Physics X-Ray Analysis Group. It appeared that she had been in touch with the British Communist Party as to whether Nunn May should be approached regarding a position in East Germany. A telephone check also revealed that she had been staying at the Woosters' in Cambridge. Nunn May had been engaged at Crystal Structures for nearly two years and the monetary support would soon come to an end. If Nunn May had met with Dornberger to discuss the offer, he might want to follow it up by visiting East Germany. If so, he would need to request a passport yet again.

What would the Government's response be? This time a memorandum on the arguments for and against refusal was drafted by Selwyn Lloyd, the Foreign Secretary, for a decision by Cabinet.

Amongst those factors in favour of granting a passport was that agreement had been reached with the Americans as regards interchange of information on atomic matters, six months previously. Security was no longer an issue since Nunn May possessed no information of value to the Russians. Consultations seemed to have taken place with John Cockcroft with whom Nunn May had worked in Canada. He did not regard Nunn May as possessing outstanding ability. Nunn May did not by law need a passport to leave the country, nor require one to return to the United Kingdom, although it would cause some difficulties. There was no legal obligation to provide one although this was unusual. There was a section of public opinion who thought that a refusal of a passport infringed the rights of an individual to freedom of movement.

MI5 expressed the view that if Nunn May did go to work behind the Iron Curtain it would bring about public criticism, whether or not he possessed a passport. MI5 were reluctant to resuscitate the subsidy to Nunn May which if it were to be revealed would bring about even greater protests from the public. The MI5 position was that Nunn May should be granted a passport subject to the views of our ambassador in Washington.

One factor against granting a passport was that Hildegarde Nunn May held Communist views as did Alan Nunn May. The question of American collaboration on atomic matters was not wholly solved by the agreements that had been signed. The British Ambassador in

Washington, Sir Roger Makins, wrote to the Foreign Secretary and expressed the view that the Americans would still be very angry about any defection by Alan Nunn May which could seriously damage expanded co-operation on atomic energy matters. The UK was heavily dependent on the USA for the supply of raw materials (e.g. Uranium 235), and information about nuclear developments for the continuation of its nuclear programme. The ambassador was strident in his letter.

> 'The effect of allowing him to go … would give the opportunity to those elements in the Congress, and also in the Commission itself, which are hostile to more extended co-operation with us and who for one reason or another wish to embarrass Admiral Strauss, to combine to defeat any further development of Anglo American co-operation in this field. You will of course realise that if such a setback were to occur, a full year would elapse before we could hope to recover lost ground. My view is that Dr May should at all costs be prevented from leaving the United Kingdom until the adjournment of Congress and such time thereafter as may be necessary…'

On 17 January 1956, the Cabinet agreed that a passport should not be granted to Alan Nunn May. It was however agreed that every effort should be made to secure him employment in the U.K. once the current arrangements with Crystal Structures ceased.

It will be remembered that MI5 managed to engineer that work whilst the efforts of the Ministry of Labour had failed. It was yet again MI5 who initiated efforts to remedy the current situation.

Dick White, Director General of MI5, wrote to Sir Frank Newsom, Permanent Under Secretary at the Home Office, saying that in his view the Nunn Mays' were settled in Cambridge and would prefer to remain there provided that Alan Nunn May received sufficient work to enable him to continue living there. Once again MI5 and the ministerial departments involved, grappled with the sensitive issue of keeping Nunn May employed in the U.K. MI5 continued to believe that Nunn May was happy to remain in the U.K. provided he could find work. They had intercepted messages suggesting that he was not enthusiastic about any offers from East Germany.

The ministries found the idea of obtaining work for him and paying for it, difficult to resolve. They were sensitive to the criticism that they were using public funds to support a former enemy of the state. They were also very uneasy in trying to cajole various industrial concerns as to the necessity of this course of action, not withstanding the problem of having to disguise funding. The general public were already asking questions about his employment at Crystal Structures. Thus the whole issue of Nunn May's employment was irritatingly back on the agenda.

The Director General of MI5 suggested to Newsom that he contact the Minister of Supply, the Lord President of the Council (responsible for the DSIR), and the President of the Board of Trade to follow through the Cabinet's decision to find Nunn May work.

Another officer of MI5, Graham Mitchell, wrote to de la Mere at the Foreign Office telling him of their requests to these government departments. He also mentioned in his correspondence that Mr Cantelo, a representative of the Ministry of Labour, and Colonel Kearn had visited Crystal Structures to see the work for themselves and to speak with Nunn May. Kearn was introduced as a non technical Higher Appointments Officer. He was in fact an officer of MI5.

Eventually Kearn was able to achieve a sort of breakthrough via a Dr Blount at the DSIR. His proposal was that Ivor Worsfold, Director of W.H. Sanders (Electronics) Ltd., might channel some of their research work through Crystal Structures specifically for Nunn May. The issue of discreet funding from public sources still remained. It was thought that funding of £1,000 per annum would suit Nunn May with an allowance for materials and equipment. The idea of inducements to private companies remained an uneasy solution and Kearn felt it would be simpler all round to grant Nunn May his funding directly from public funds for a three year period and that this be disguised in some way. Kearn made the point that Nunn May could apply for the grant directly to the DSIR, but the details could be discreetly hidden.

Two years later on 28 July 1958, Alan Nunn May applied for a passport again. He said that he wanted to go to Austria on holiday and that the reasons given in the past for refusing him were now no longer valid.

Again Selwyn Lloyd, in a memorandum to his Cabinet colleagues, went over the history behind the refusal to grant him a passport. This time he was able to add further information about how Nunn May was conducting his life in the UK. He seemed to be putting down roots. Recently he had bought an annuity and was paying instalments on another. He had taken out an education policy for the benefit of his son and was interested in buying a house.

The intermediary from East Germany who had offered him employment in 1956, had visited the UK but had made no contact with him.

There had been a new agreement with the United States on the exchange of atomic information. This would be completed in August, Congress would be in recess, and the previous considerations of 1956 which had resulted in a refusal to issue a passport were considerably diminished. There were no security or scientific objections to Nunn May travelling abroad.

During this period a telephone check was maintained on Nunn May's address in Cambridge and on his place of work at Crystal Structures. This appears to have been a somewhat off and on arrangement. The amount of information it provided was limited and MI5 appeared to realise that Nunn May was probably aware that his telephone calls were being monitored and was careful about what he said. An example of this was after a telephone engineer had been to repair the telephone, the Nunn May's joked in one of their conversations that their newly adopted son Johnnie had probably played with the telephone. Hildegarde's son from her first marriage, Paul, had suggested he take a screwdriver and investigate the receiving device.

Selwyn Lloyd recommended that once the new agreement with the United States had been completed and Congress was in recess, a passport could be issued to Nunn May.

On 12 August 1958, Selwyn Lloyd's Memorandum was discussed at Cabinet, the Prime Minister, Harold Macmillan was in the Chair. Those present were; Viscount Kilmuir, Lord Chancellor; the Earl of Home, Secretary of State for Commonwealth Relations; Duncan Sandys, Minister of Defence; Harold Watkinson, Minister of Transport; D.

Heathcoat Amory, Chancellor of the Exchequer; Viscount Hailsham, Lord President of the Council; Sir David Eccles, President of the Board of Trade; John Hare, Minister of Agriculture, Fisheries and Food; Charles Hill, Chancellor of the Duchy of Lancaster; David Ormsby Gore, Minister of State for Foreign Affairs; the Earl of Perth, Minister of State for Colonial Affairs; and Sir Frederick Hoyer Millar of the Foreign Office.

They were informed that the Home Office supported the application as did the Security Services. They believed that Nunn May had established himself in this country and had no intention of leaving it permanently. Neither did they believe he had any intention of seeking asylum in the Soviet Union or its satellite states.

The Cabinet remained divided on the issue.

Again the posibilty of being embarrassed by adverse reaction from the United States, and the general public was still seen as being relevant, particularly if Nunn May sought refuge behind the Iron Curtain. The other argument put was that the embarrassment would be worse if he was not granted a passport and chose to go because of the government's intransigence in insisting that he must be prevented from doing so. After all he did not need a passport to do so. He should be granted a passport and the United States Government told that this had been done because he no longer held secret information of value to a potential enemy.

The Prime Minister summed up by saying that Nunn May should not be given facilities for foreign travel until the conclusion of the atomic energy agreements with the United States.

The Foreign Secretary was asked to arrange for Nunn May to be informed that a passport would not be granted to him during the course of 1958.

Six months later on Tuesday 17 February 1959, the Cabinet had before it yet another request from Nunn May for the granting of a passport. He still wanted to take that holiday in Austria.

The meeting chaired by the Prime Minister, Harold Macmillan, was reminded of the history surrounding Nunn May's request for a passport by the Parliamentary Under Secretary of State for Foreign

Affairs, Mr R.A. Allan. He said that the negotiations for the exchange of nuclear information and materials had been considered by the Ambassador in Washington to be at risk if Nunn May was granted a passport. The Foreign Secretary said that there was always going to be some risk of embarrassment, and felt that the time had come for his passport application to be granted. In discussion, it was reported that Nunn May seemed to have established a permanent home in this country, he was no longer involved in undesirable political activities and therefore there was no undue danger in granting him a passport.

The Cabinet invited the Home Secretary in consultation with the Foreign Secretary to ascertain whether Nunn May was involved in any subversive political activity. If this revealed nothing, he should be granted a passport.

At the Cabinet meeting on 26 February 1959, with Mr R.A. Butler in the Chair, the Foreign Secretary confirmed that Nunn May was no longer involved in subversive activities. The Cabinet agreed that the application for a passport by Dr Alan Nunn May should now be granted.

It had required five attempts since 1954 to achieve a successful outcome. He was now at last, a free man to travel as he wished.

EPILOGUE

In January 1962, Alan Nunn May secured a post as Research Professor of Physics at the University of Ghana in Accra. This had been the result of an approach by President Kwame Nkrumah. Ghana was a newly independent state and no longer part of the British Empire. He ultimately served as Dean of the Faculty of Science from 1964–1969. He set up the Solid State and Metal Physics Research Group in 1962 to train young Ghanaian scientists in the physics of solids. This included research work on the origin of diamonds in the earth's crust.

His wife went with him and she developed a reputation as a tireless medical worker in that country. Alan Nunn May retired in 1978 and returned to live in Cambridge.

There was to be one further act of disclosure. Shortly before he died, he prepared a statement which was made public after his death. In it he revealed that he had been passing information to the Russians since 1941 (no names were revealed), twelve months before signing up to join Tube Alloys Research in 1942 and signing the Official Secrets Act. He admitted that he was motivated by the need to ensure that Russia, which had been invaded by Nazi Germany, was not left behind in the race to acquire nuclear weapons. He admitted to supplying large quantities of information as the atom bomb became a reality, and that this was not for financial gain but in support of his personal ideology. He maintained that at the time he was passing information, there had been a treaty which allowed the sharing of information between allies.

At his trial he had pleaded guilty in order to conceal how many years he had been passing information and avoid incriminating others, in particular the Russian spy network in the United Kingdom. He also accepted that the advent of the Cold War set the general public against him and was to affect his subsequent treatment. Nowhere in his statement was anyone named nor was there any expression of regret.

Alan Nunn May died in Cambridge on 12 January 2003.

ACKNOWLEDGMENTS

I am indebted to Sheila Parker of Barnt Green who first mentioned the name Alan Nunn May to me, and his association with Barnt Green, and his family's link with the house I currently live in. As a serving member of the WRNS, she had worked during World War II at Bletchley Park and was instrumental in my researching this story.

I am grateful to Anne Bradford for her encouragement to pursue publication of this material. Also to Alison Wheatley, Archivist at King Edward VI School, Edgbaston Birmingham; Dr George K. Nkrumah-Buandoh, Department of Physics, University of Ghana; Dr David Temperton, Head of RRPPS, for his advice on nuclear physics; Benjamin Rouben, Canadian Nuclear Society for the supply of a photograph of the staff at the Montreal Laboratory. John Hirons for his computing advice to keep my documentation safe.

Finally and most importantly to the National Archives, Kew, Richmond, Surrey, without whose documented records this book would not have been possible.

BIBLIOGRAPHY

Andrew, Christopher: *The Defence of the Realm*, Allen Lane 2000

Boyle, Andrew: *The Climate of Treason*, Hutchinson 1979

Broda, Paul: *Scientist Spies. A Memoir Of My Three Parents and The Atom Bomb*, Troubador 2011

Box, Muriel: *Rebel Advocate – A Biography of Gerald Gardiner*, Victor Gollancz Ltd 1983

Dulles, Allen: *Great True Spy Stories – The Iron Curtain by Igor Gouzenko*, Collins.

Howarth, T.E.B.: *Cambridge Between Two Wars*, Collins 1978

Muggeridge, Malcolm: *The Thirties*, Collins 1967

West, Rebecca: *The Meaning of Treason*, The Reprint Society Ltd., 1952

Wright, Peter: *Spycatcher*, Viking Penguin 1987

Articles

Laurence, George: *Early Years of Nuclear Energy Research in Canada*, Atomic Energy of Canada, 1980

Igor Gouzenko: *Camp X Historical Society*, P.O. Box 23, Whitby, Ontario, Canada, L1N 5R7

Bertrand Goldschmidt: *How it All Began in Canada – The Role of the French Scientists*, Canadian Nuclear Society.

References

The National Archives of the UK (TNA)
Public Record Office (PRO)
KV 2/2209– 2226; KV 2553–2555; KV 2/2563–2564.
CAB 128/25–26; CAB 128/32–33; CAB 128/40; CAB 129/57; CAB 129/79; CAB 129/94; CAB 195/11; CAB 195/14.